THE 10 Ms OF MONEY

- Why we lose money - motives, mindsets and mistakes
- How we make money - making, managing, multiplying, magnetising it
- The God factor - mandate, ministry and miracle of money
- Total freedom from financial hardship

MATTHEW ASHIMOLOWO

© 2003 Matthew Ashimolowo
Published by Mattyson Media an imprint of MAMM
Matthew Ashimolowo Media Ministries

Visit our website: www.pastormatthew.tv

ISBN 1 874646 61 9

2nd Edition, Third Printing 2017

Bible quotes are from the King James version Bible unless otherwise stated. The New Living Translation, The Amplified Bible, The Message Translation, The Living Bible, The Bible in Basic English, The Modern Language Bible: The New Berkeley Version in Modern English

P. 201 quoted from "Webster's Dictionary of the English Language - The Encyclopedic edition" ; P. 249 quoted from "Webster's Dictionary"; P. 261 quoted from "Webster's Dictionary" P. 216 quoted from "101 Great Laws of Success" Matthew Ashimolowo

CONTENTS

INTRODUCTION

As we draw close to the end of times and as we advance the gospel in this third millennium, the time has come for us to fully understand and to maximise the days and opportunities that God has given us. The time has come for us to understand the power of the wealthy place, which Christ's redemptive work has provided. Not only to understand, but to operate in that wealthy place.

> *Thou hast caused men to ride over our heads; we went through fire and through water: but thou broughtest us out into a wealthy place. Psalm 66:12*

The church has had its dance and shouts for a long time, but we have to come to the table with the financial decision makers of this world so that we can possess the blessing available to us. The time has come for the church to be empowered to do the things it was ordained for. The time has come for us to come freely into all that was set aside for us, so that it can be exposed to us by revelation and intuition.

> *That the blessing of Abraham might come on the Gentiles through Jesus Christ; that we might receive the promise of the Spirit through faith. Galatians 3:14*

God's invitation to us is to live in the wealthy place; a place with people who will help us to be a people after His own kind. If God put the seed producing after its own kind in everything else, He put the seed of creativity in you because you are His image.

Some might wonder, why a book about money? Martin Luther King said, "Any religion that claims to be concerned about people without addressing the economic conditions that strangle them is a dry and useless religion." The time has come for us to use the anointing upon us to create an economic bridge over the deprivation, stagnation and poverty that seems to hold many church people down. Let us face it, the economics in which the majority of church people have found themselves seem to be set to create deliberate stagnation in our community.

Here in Europe we hear of European monies, new deals and big deals, but these deals have not broken the power of poverty in the community in which we find ourselves.

Is there a certain part of the poverty and deprivation that is deliberate and planned? It seems so, and only the power of the kingdom of God can break this satanic system that seems to be enslaving God's people a second time when the Word of the Lord says,

> What do ye imagine against the LORD? he will make an utter end: affliction shall not rise up the second time. Nahum 1:9

There seems to be a design that enriches a few by the labour and resources of many. And the many who are enriching the few happen to be in our community. This seems like an oxymoron since we are meant to be the head and not the tail. However, you can only go to war with the weapons you have. It is time for us to truly wake up and occupy our wealthy place, but we must have the financial know-how.

Economic deprivation is basically the fact that the wealth produced by the labour of the masses is controlled by the few, and most times these few are unsaved people. There is a lot of talk about supply and demand. The only problem is that we are in the demand sector. That must change because we are ordained to create wealth and if a man does not know his ordination he will be outside the programme of God. If you do not know your blessing you will end up begging. If you do not have the financial and economic know-how, you will take whatever is put on your table. Christians must know who they are and what their worth is in God.

We must know in the Christian community that there cannot be appropriation of wealth until you know the source and style of generational wealth. By reason of your 'God connection' you were created, saved and delivered to live in the wealthy place. This means that poverty is no longer your native language and your culture, and poverty is not your calling. The production and distribution of good things is not on the basis of race, face or place, and if you do not know what you are called to, you will let people define where you operate in life.

God ordained Zion to be a place for the outflow of wisdom. The church of the last days is meant to be efficient economically, inspirationally, comprehensively and substantially so that it can do more than it has ever done.

Until you learn to live and walk in your wealthy place a person leads you and has the papers to the house you think belongs to you. You spend the next 25 to 30 years serving a mortgage (or 50 years if you live in Japan).

The place where this book challenges you to rise up to is beyond having more than enough. It is where you can have enough to make an impact on your generation. Being wise is not enough; you ought to be wise and blessed for you to be a blessing and to be remembered.

Now there was found in it a poor wise man, and he by his wisdom delivered the city; yet no man remembered that same poor man. Ecclesiastes 9:15

Why is the world not listening to us? Why do they take the church for granted and think we cannot bring the answer? Because the economic world has a method of listening to those who have an answer and to those who made the policies. The ungodly that have, are killing the morality of our generation because they buy up television and radio channels, newspapers and all media for communicating their own opinion. They pick on the church and 'eat the church for breakfast,' but we do not have enough to counter the ungodly philosophy they dish out.

The goal of this book is not for a casual visit but a whole life. It is a call for you to create wealth for the coming generations to benefit and be blessed. The greatest form of poverty is to use everything you have in one generation. The reason God gives ideas and businesses is so that you can perpetuate what your grandchildren will enjoy.

This book calls you to another choice for the Christian life. The choice for you to open yourself to be blessed financially so that you can make an impact, or else you will watch the enemies of the cross do all the trade, take control, take charge, determine where you live, how you live and what you wear. It is a call for you not to allow the devourer to eat up everything you have in one generation.

The word devourer means 'seed eater', debt or devil. Is there a devourer in the land? Take Britain for example, 80 per cent of the British people owe more than they can pay and more than they earn. In Britain, at retirement, 90 per cent cannot write a cheque. Nine out of ten people in the British society have to wait for a pay cheque. Remember we are talking about the first world, one of the G8 countries.

Sixty per cent are borrowing above their own ability and many would be on the street if they did not mortgage their house. A mortgaged house basically means that you work for 25 years serving a loan and paying for a house that does not belong to you. Although it carries your name, you never see the paper.

Within the black community in the United Kingdom 90 per cent of those who die are without a will, so all the money that you worked hard for goes back to the government. Many on the other hand live all their life just paying tax. Talking about tax, you actually pay it four times; when you earn, spend, save or die.

Many Christians have really allowed the spirit of the age to conform them; it is time to be transformed to live in the wealthy place.

I beseech you therefore, brethren, by the mercies of God, that ye present your bodies a living sacrifice, holy, acceptable unto God, which is your reasonable service. And be not conformed to this world: but be ye transformed by the renewing of your mind, that ye may prove what is that good, and acceptable, and perfect, will of God. Rom.12:1-2

It is time for us to occupy our place in the programme of God. The wealthy place, as has been mentioned several times, is a place chosen before the foundation of the world.

But with the precious blood of Christ, as of a lamb without blemish and without spot: Who verily was foreordained before the foundation of the world, but was manifest in these last times for you, 1 Peter 1:19-20

And all that dwell upon the earth shall worship him, whose names are not written in the book of life of the Lamb slain from the foundation of the world. Revelation 13:8

Jesus fully paid for you to occupy such a place. Already the extent of God's provision for us for the wealthy place is seen in the book of Isaiah.

Oh, that You would rend the heavens! That You would come down! That the mountains might shake at Your presence. As fire burns brushwood, as fire causes water to boil—To make Your name known to Your adversaries, that the nations may tremble at Your presence! When You did awesome things for which we did not look, You came down, the mountains shook at Your presence. For since the beginning of the world Men have not heard nor perceived by the ear, Nor has the eye seen any God besides You, Who acts for the one who waits for Him. Isaiah 64:1-4

Provision was made before sin was known; therefore it is a place of abundance. It is a place that belongs to you, where you will come into a wealth of relationships, wisdom, vision, money and mission. It is a place of unspeakable joy and that is full of glory; the place where we are able to praise God in spite of what provisions we have because it helps us to carry out our purpose. It is a place of honour before all the nations of the earth where good and great things   happen.

And it shall be to me a name of joy, a praise and an honour before all the nations of the earth, which shall hear all the good that I do unto them: and they shall fear and tremble for all the goodness and for all the prosperity that I procure unto it. Jeremiah 33:9

The human mind cannot comprehend it. It is where you enter and divine insight, brilliant ideas, visions and favours begin to flow. This is the life and calling fore-ordained for those who know Christ.

For we are God's [own] handiwork (his workmanship), re-created in Christ Jesus, [born anew] that we may do those good works which God predestined (planned beforehand) for us [taking paths which He prepared ahead of time], that we should walk in them [living the good life which He prearranged and made ready for us to live]. Ephesians 2:10 (Amplified)

The word 'create' or 're-create' in this verse means 'to find the path again which was once lost'. That path means that it is the steps that will lead us to the place of God's favour. The path is the path of learning to sow seed so it can bring you there; blessing the poor, honouring your parents with that which He provides for you, blessing a prophet of God, bringing your first fruit and learning wisdom principles for investment.

The paths are: learning when to sow seed and learning when to get involved in a business. The answer is not struggle, but a discovery of what has been fixed.

> *But thou shalt remember the LORD thy God: for it is he that giveth thee power to get wealth, that he may establish his covenant which he sware unto thy fathers, as it is this day. Deuteronomy 8:18*

The law is coming out of Zion and the glory of Zion will soon be revealed.

-1-
THE MISTAKES

Did you know that upon the birth of a baby if you start saving £100 a month for the baby in a compounded interest account, by the time the baby is 25 you are likely to have £1 million?

Did you know that if you turn your £1.50, money spent towards coffee every day, to savings, at the end of 40 years of work, you are likely to have almost £0.5 million if it is put in a high interest account?

Did you know that a person who starts working at the age of 25 and saves £100 a month in a compounded interest account for the next 40 years of work is likely to have £1 million handed to him?

These and many others are the results when we choose not to make money mistakes but to manage effectively what God has provided for us. There are several money mistakes that we could refer to. However, for the sake of space, we will confine ourselves to about 22.

1. GET RICH QUICK SCHEMES

He that hasteth to be rich hath an evil eye, and considereth not that poverty shall come upon him. Proverbs 28:22

The lack of money makes people begin to want to accelerate their years and try to cover for the days they have lost by trying to look for a quick way to make money.

Their action is prompted by the saying that opportunity knocks but once. However, it is what is secured by labour that increases. Productive ideas are the assets any business exploit must have in order to make progress. So if one believes in a 'get rich quick' system, it will not take long before someone realises that your belief can make you either a victor or a victim, and in the case of 'get rich quick' schemes, *"A fool and his money may soon be parted."*

As you will find later on in the chapter 'The Magnet', some people repel money while others attract it. Let us look closely at some of the actions that result in money mistakes and make people to repel money.

2. IGNORANCE OF THE BIBLICAL COVENANT OF PROSPERITY

But thou shalt remember the LORD thy God: for it is he that giveth thee power to get wealth, that he may establish his covenant which he sware unto thy fathers, as it is this day. Deuteronomy 8:18

Deuteronomy 8:18 establishes the fact that God gives us power to prosper and to establish His covenant with us.

3. THE BELIEF THAT THERE IS A CONSPIRACY TO KEEP YOU POOR

One of the worst excuses for being poor is the belief that there is a conspiracy by the wealthy to keep people perpetually poor. On the contrary, the poor themselves carry out actions that keep them perpetually in that state. Imagine our opening statement, the fact that if you save £1.50 in a high interest account every day, it would multiply into hundreds of thousands of pounds.

4. THE BELIEF THAT CURRENCY IS SOMETHING HARD TO EARN

In certain poor nations, western currencies are referred to as hard currency, failing to realise that your confession becomes your possession. If you call it 'hard to get' or 'hard currency', it really becomes what you called it. Money is a neutral instrument of exchange. It respects and goes where it is attracted. Money is not hard to earn, the only problem on earth is a wisdom problem. Money comes if you find a problem and solve it.

5. DEVELOPING 'FRUIT EATER' MENTALITY AND NOT THAT OF A 'SEED SOWER'

People stay perpetually poor when they fail to realise that it is a mistake not to release. Giving is living, giving provokes receiving, releasing is your access way to increasing. If you develop a 'fruit eater' mentality, it means in effect that you have not learnt the power of seed sowing. Farmers are known to reserve the best seed of their harvest for the next planting. Those with the 'fruit eater' mentality have the habit of thinking, "Why save when you can spend?"

6. BELIEVING THAT A GOOD JOB IS A SOURCE OF CREATING PROSPERITY

The acronym JOB stands for 'Just Over Broke'. Having a job is better than being unemployed. However, if we must make kingdom impact on the economy of the world, we must go beyond getting a good job. It is a money mistake to just be a job seeker.

7. SAVING BUT NOT SAVING SMARTLY

Some people's idea of saving is hiding money in places for rainy days; so they keep money in cookie jars, under the pillow and other obscure places; otherwise some people's bank account would only attract an interest rate which is lower than the inflationary rate of their country.

8. IRRESPONSIBLE USE OF RESOURCES

Every source of money that comes into your hand is used either for downward or upward investments. Downward investment is when your resources are used irresponsibly for the things that do not duplicate, replicate or multiply themselves. If your outgoings are more than your incomings, it is an irresponsible use of money.

9. TRYING TO GET RICH QUICK

This certainly is a major money mistake because it sows the seed of dishonesty and provokes actions that may come back to haunt you.

10. WITHHOLDING BENEVOLENCE

There is that scattereth, and yet increaseth; and there is that withholdeth more than is meet, but it tendeth to poverty. Proverbs 11:24

11. CHEATING

A false balance is abomination to the Lord: but a just weight is His delight. Proverbs 11:1

Cheating is when you want to take more than you deserve and coveting what belongs to someone else. Once you have a mind to cheat, you desire to over-profit. It is a money mistake to think that by cheating you can increase.

12. REFUSING TO TRY AGAIN BECAUSE OF PREVIOUS FAILURE

One of the characteristics of the wealthy is not that they make £100 per cent good financial decisions, but rather that when they make bad financial decisions and sometimes have lost everything. They have formed belief systems: habits, actions and attitudes that make them stay in the fight until failure is reversed and turned to success.

13. DOWNWARD INVESTMENT INSTEAD OF UPWARD INVESTMENT

We have made reference to this earlier. It is spending money on things that depreciate. If the value of your car is higher than the value of your house, it is a downward investment. If there is more going towards clothes for your back than savings for your future and your children, it is a downward investment. Clothes have never been known to appreciate, and neither do cars. Cars only depreciate. In third world nations the currency tends to fall in comparison to major currencies like the Dollar and the British Pound Sterling.

14. LATENT BELIEF THAT ONLY GREEDY PEOPLE CAN BE BLESSED

The word 'blessed' means to be empowered. Abraham was not greedy, he was a giver and he was blessed. Jesus' definition of blessing shows that it can come upon anyone who can trust God enough.

Blessed and fortunate and happy and spiritually prosperous (in that state in which the born-again child of God enjoys His favour and salvation) are those who hunger and thirst for righteousness (uprightness and right standing with God), for they shall be completely satisfied! Blessed (happy, to be envied, and spiritually prosperous-- with life-joy and satisfaction in God's favour and salvation, regardless of their outward conditions) are the merciful, for they shall obtain mercy! Matthew 5:6-7 (Amplified)

If your belief system is wrong, it is going to affect what you receive.

15. BLAMING POVERTY ON THE LACK OF CAPITAL FOR STARTING OFF

Knowledge is capital and an asset. The skill you have acquired over your lifetime is an asset, the experiences you have had are assets. Your ability to have survived seasons of lack is an asset in itself for making progress into abundance.

16. MYTHICAL STATEMENTS THAT WE HOLD ONTO

There are several of such statements like, "I was not born under a lucky star." Nobody was, everyone had to start from somewhere. Or, "It is not what you know but whom you know." To blame lack on the absence of contacts and to think that prosperity comes because of a big brother situation is to strangulate your own future. "I was not born with a silver spoon in my mouth." A study shows that 30 per cent of American millionaires were self-made who never inherited wealth. Another survey showed in the book "The Millionaire Next Door," that immigrants are more likely to become millionaires faster than those who have always lived in the US.

17. REFUSING TO TAKE RISKS AND INVESTING

The Chinese say, "He who is afraid to throw the dice will never throw a six". Once you are afraid to invest you limit your ability to come into the blessing of God. If you do not deal with your money fears they will hold you down, hold you back and make you to never come into all that God has for you.

18. THE BELIEF THAT "BIG BROTHER," THE GOVERNMENT, OWES YOU

In my travels around the world, one of the characteristics of many poor nations is that people are often looking up to the government to be their saviour from financial traps. It is apparent to anyone with enough sense to see that some people are lazy and at the same time resourceful and gifted, yet they will do nothing but sit down all day and blame the government which itself does not know how to emancipate its people from economic deprivation. It may be hard to say but a people only get the Government they deserve.

Living in the United Kingdom and seeing people draw social benefits instead of working sometimes makes me feel like they have given themselves to economic slavery. There are those, of course, who by reason of a loss of their job, due to old age or sickness, should draw such benefits. However, there are the strong and healthy who sit down and wait for 'Big Brother.'

19. PREFERRING PERSONAL COMFORT TO THE PROGRESS OF GOD'S WORK.

Is it time for you, o ye, to dwell in your ceiled houses, and this house lie waste? Haggai 1:4

How can you trust and pray to God to prosper you when you withhold from the same One whom you expect to bless you. Withholding the tithe and offerings affect the work of God. The tithe in particular, when it is touched means that we have stolen from the One who should bless us.

Ye are cursed with a curse: for you have robbed me, even this whole nation. Bring ye all the tithes into the storehouse, that there may be meat in mine house, and prove me now herewith, saith the Lord of hosts, if I will not open you the windows of heaven, and pour you out a blessing, that there shall not be room enough to receive it. Malachi 3: 9-10

20. LIVING A MONEY-CENTERED LIFE

It is a mistake to live a money-centered life because your identity is not in money but God. Those who have chosen to make how much they have or do not have determine their joy, easily become frustrated because they allow what can change and what is influenced by the constant change in the economy to affect their life.

21. IRRESPONSIBLE USE OF RESOURCES

The wise stewardship of limited resources can make you

earn more in life, but once you begin to incur debts, buy on the basis of impulse, or carelessly manage what has been provided for you, you draw yourself into major money mistakes and you become perpetually in financial trouble and debt.

22. Indebtedness

Of all the money mistakes, the most major for the modern man is going into debt. There are people who spend 20 per cent of their income servicing the debt they have. They cannot afford to be without a job or a business. In the words of the poor: "I owe, I owe and so to work I go."

We will cover indebtedness more closely. However, once you launch yourself on an ocean of red ink, buying things you cannot pay for and having lines of credit for everything, it means you are living beyond your means and are spending the money you have not earned.

Indebtedness is often rooted in a person's sense of compulsion to buy, and with today's easy availability of credit facilities people see what they like, and because the price seems right they bring out their credit cards and buy, unknown to them that they may be clearing the path to poverty. Going into debt is an indirect training for your children to follow the same.

The rich ruleth over the poor, and the borrower is servant to the lender. Proverbs 22:7

In the previous verse the Bible says, "To train up a child in the way he should go."

Train up a child in the way he should go: and when he is old, he will not depart from it. Proverbs 22:6

So your child observes you and sees your actions. Borrowing is the father of bankruptcy. Once it is not controlled, bankruptcy will look you in the face. Indebtedness is an evil spirit that has your destruction as its ultimate goal. Those who provide credit facilities prefer you to borrow because it helps the economy and helps their own income. So that the car you were supposed to buy for £15,000, you might end up paying £21,000 at the end of four or five years.

Debtors are presumptuous that they will have a job tomorrow.

In today's volatile world that is a tall order. Debt makes Christians forget that they are promise keepers and so when they are unable to fulfil their promise, excuses are given and sometimes lies are told to cover their tracks.

A greater per cent of those that draw the equity on their house often use it to pay off debts they owe; whereas those who create wealth will take the equity to start a new business or buy more real estate.

You cannot really overcome indebtedness unless you are realistic about your income and how much of it is available to you. Imagine a man who earns £12,000 and pays 25 per cent in tax, 7 per cent in national insurance, 17.5 per cent value added tax on all purchases except for the children's clothing and a few of the necessities we buy. In a nutshell, out of 12 months income only eight months income really stays with you. So if you earn £12,000, what is really available to you is £8,000.

Remember also that out of the £8,000, £1,200 belongs to the Lord in the tithe. This leaves the believer with £6,800. Ignorance of these facts will make indebtedness spread faster than any disease, it will make such a person groan every time they want to give to God because they calculate what 10 per cent (the tithe) now means to them forgetting that the Government did not ask permission before it withdrew its own 32 per cent in income tax and national insurance contributions.

Indebtedness makes some well-meaning couples struggle in spite of the level of wages they earn.

Having bought most of the things in their house on credit, unpaid bills now stay on their mind like a bad dream. They walk on carpets that are 'buy now pay later', they drive a car that is on a similar arrangement, their home is mortgaged, the television they watch is bought on credit, they patronise catalogues and brochures of shopping companies that allow you to buy and spread the payment over years. The result is family tension and constant arguments.

Indebtedness also drains the joy out of payday.

It has meant that some people have eaten the tithe and money that belongs to God. Lies and deception are easier for debtors than those who are debt free. Confidence is eroded when you are a debtor, particularly when you see the people you owe. Indebtedness makes you enslaved to the system of the world.

The Word says, "borrowers are servants of lenders." The major reason for work then becomes paying all your lenders, ensuring that you keep them happy so they do not come and use the long arm of the law to take everything you have. Most western nations have so empowered lenders to recover their money by using the long arm of the law, even if it means throwing you out of your accommodation and repossessing everything you have worked for to pay off the money you owe.

Indebtedness may cause the courts to determine what you spend your money on, in other words a counsellor may have to be hired to budget your own income for you, and such a counsellor may decide that you have no right to bring the tithe. The 'buy now pay later' marketing strategy of this world enslaves you and your children.

Of course there is the time to use debt but only as leverage for a business so that you are using other people's money to perpetuate and produce more money. As a result, your children are being raised in the atmosphere of debt and when you bring up your children as debtors, you have disobeyed the Lord.

Train up a child in the way he should go: and when he is old, he will not depart from it. Proverbs 22:6

Children catch behaviours and children also go forth and perpetuate what they have seen you do. Borrowing is the guaranteed passport to financial slavery. The rich rule over the poor and the borrower is servant to the lender.

The rich ruleth over the poor, and the borrower is servant to the lender. Proverbs 22:7

Unless there is a change, generation upon generation will be held in financial bondage. So while the righteous man leaves an inheritance for his grandchildren, the debtor leaves challenges, battles and heartache for their spouse and relations.

A good man leaveth an inheritance to his children's children; and the wealth of the sinner is laid up for the just. Proverbs 13:22

Now there cried a certain woman of the wives of the sons of the prophets unto Elisha, saying, Thy servant my husband is dead; and thou knowest that thy servant did fear the Lord; and the creditor is come to take unto him my two sons to be bondmen. 2 Kings 4:1

The indebtedness of the prophet, which he left for his wife and sons, added burdens, multiplied their worries, subtracted their peace and divided their minds.

He now left his wife worried because the only thing he left in the world for her, her sons, were about to be taken by the people who provided the credit facilities.

Indebtedness produces sleepless nights and makes people question your integrity. It makes you feel the grind of borrowing on the inside. Indebtedness embarrasses you particularly when you are behind in your payments. It can lead to family acrimony. Indebtedness makes you not look forward to the postman bringing your letters because another reminder might be on the way.

Indebtedness invites the spirit of fear into your home so that you are no longer at peace but perpetually afraid of what might happen to you and your family.

Indebtedness takes away confidence and makes the man feel inadequate as a provider for his family. Indebtedness leaves your family stressed because any little wastage by your children makes you over-react over 'spilled milk.'

Debt between friends is another great challenge that causes the separation of friends. Imagine borrowing your friend's car and just as you were coming back from your trip, someone who was driving dented a part of it. Having no money to repair it, you had to take it and explain. The reaction of the friend immediately changes because what is important to them has been tampered with. The spirit of debt is a bad master; it rules and it ruins.

Indebtedness can frustrate the vision of a church.

People have been tempted to steal, therefore losing their job or even facing the possibility of a jail sentence because of indebtedness. Technically, the lender determines the movement of a borrower. They determine where you may go, what you may do and how you may spend. So when a debtor is led by the Holy Spirit to give a certain amount, the first thing he remembers is his line of credit which must not be jeopardised and so he faces the temptation of disobeying the Holy Spirit thus being rendered useless in the promotion of the kingdom of God with his income.

Indebtedness really does frustrate one's destiny because the calling on the believer is to go out and make money in order to use it to promote the kingdom of God. However, the rich who rule over the poor are now taking it.

People who get into indebtedness presume or forecast the future. They presume that the current value of their house is a certain amount and is likely to increase. They fail to realise that things could happen and there could be calamities or disasters in the area where they live.

In summary debt is a thief that robs one of his time and life. It is like being enslaved again to serve people you owe. It is the transfer of the wealth of the poor to the wealthy. Somebody somewhere is spending your money because you have chosen to walk in indebtedness. So if you cannot imagine Jesus in debt, then it is not the lifestyle you should follow.

23. OVER COMMITMENT TO CAREER

You become distinguished in your chosen field, however, when you are married to your business or job imbalance become inevitable. Everything around you hurts; including your marriage and your relationship with God.

No man that warreth entangleth himself with the affairs of this life; that he may please him who hath chosen him to be a soldier. 2 Timothy 2:4

The money you make from such a business or career becomes   tainted.

24. INVESTMENT HANG-UPS

Once in a while people have had the opportunity to invest and some have taken the path of doing nothing. This is a money mistake. Below are the following ideas some people have:

People do not invest because they tend to look for horror stories that confirm the negative hypothesis they hold on investment. They know of the person who invested and all the money went down the drain. However, we must remember that life has its own elements of risk. We take risks every day.

However if they are the risks that help us make progress it is another matter altogether. Driving is a risk, sitting on a chair is a risk, getting out of bed is a risk - you might be stepping out and not even know that you are in danger. Living in a multi-storey building is a risk. Life is full of risks; it is just that one should know which ones he takes.

People do not invest because they are busy comparing themselves to those who are not doing as well as they are. Lockstep mentality holds many people below their ability. They have 'HIV'. 'HIV' here means Having Insufficient Vision. Your vision is not proportionate to somebody else's. You might have been called to go further, achieve more and do greater things.

People do not invest because they believe that a negative prediction of finance will be fulfilled soon. There have always been predictions about how investments would do and as a matter of fact even if the economy takes a downturn, and the stock exchange goes "AWOL" (Absent Without Leave), it is during economic hardships and bad times that certain people take the risk that makes them prosper.

Some take risks when the value of their stocks are going down. They delay instead of cutting their losses; they hold on and hope for a comeback. While on one hand we talk of risk, yet on another it would be unwise to risk everything one has in the face of apparent loss. There might be the time when you will have to count your losses and minimise it.

Some people's reaction to an investment opportunity is too slow, too little, and too late. Procrastination does not only steal time, it steals money, the future, and opportunities. Which one of us does not remember certain business opportunities and real estates that were proposed to us and we did nothing on time or when it was time to react, it was a late reaction?

The fear of losing and the fear of regret often make people not take action and invest. One of the characteristics of those who breakthrough in business is the ability to invest and follow through. Sometimes they lose but having formed the habit of investing and pursuing hard, they would rather be afraid of the pain of inaction than the consequence of a loss.

25. MEASURING YOUR LIFE BY MATERIAL THINGS ONLY, IS A MONEY MISTAKE.

It is a money mistake to measure your life purely by your income, savings or the amount of money you have. Your intellect, skills and the abilities of God residing in you are assets.

26. MAKING YOUR FINANCIAL WELLBEING DEPENDENT ON OTHERS

Making your financial well being dependent on someone else's action fully reflects the mindset of the poor. It is limiting because it holds your destiny and ties it to the progress other people make. This is what characterises organisations and makes life harder for those at the lower cadre of the system so that when there is need to shed staff the poorly paid are the first to go.

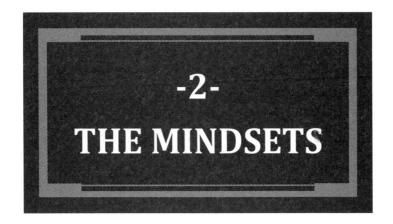

-2-
THE MINDSETS

The human mind is an incredible template that basically records and carries out and prints out whatever we have chosen it to. There is a kingdom mindset, a rich or wealthy mindset, a poor man's mindset and there is the mind of Christ.

Let this mind be in you, which was also in Christ Jesus: Philippians 2:5

This scripture shows us that though He is equal with God, Jesus chose to humble Himself. However, that did not take away His sense of value. There is a mindset which the wealthy have and it is that mindset that influences what they do. So sometimes, by reasons of calamity, adversity, misfortune or challenges, the wealthy have lost their wealth, but because they have a mindset that seeks the creation of wealth, they are able to re-create it.

There is a kingdom mindset that influences the perspective of the believer while he lives on this planet.

Our study in this chapter is primarily on the mindset of the poor. What is poverty? Poverty is the absence of everything that makes a man's life happy and comfortable. It is the shortage of supply in   certain areas where a need is expressed. As it relates to this book, it is where there is the shortage of financial supply.

The Bible refers to poverty in grades: poor, poorer and poorest. The deeper a person steps into poverty, the greater the impact on the person's life and that of generations to come. Three scriptures show us levels of poverty.

Poor

For the poor always ye have with you; but me ye have not always. John 12:8

Poorer

But if he be poorer than thy estimation, then he shall present himself before the priest, and the priest shall value him; according to his ability that vowed shall the priest value him. Leviticus 27:8

Poorest

And he carried away all Jerusalem, and all the princes, and all the mighty men of valour, even ten thousand captives, and all the craftsmen and smiths: none remained, save the poorest sort of the people of the land. 2 Kings 24:14

How come in Psalm 66: 12 it says that God brought us out and into a wealthy place? Yet Christians still struggle? Why do people still struggle with poverty and are unable to break free from its power?

Thou hast caused men to ride over our heads; we went through fire and through water: but thou broughtest us out into a wealthy place. Psalm 66:12

It is impossible to break free from a problem, a fetter or a bondage until you fully appreciate its magnitude and hindrance in your life. You cannot overcome what you are not willing to confront. Christians have sometimes chosen not to confront poverty but make room for it.

WHAT IS POVERTY?

Poverty and lack are a curse of the law.

But it shall come to pass, if thou wilt not hearken unto the voice of the LORD thy God, to observe to do all his commandments and his statutes which I command thee this day; that all these curses shall come upon thee, and overtake thee: Deuteronomy 28:15

He shall lend to thee, and thou shalt not lend to him: he shall be the head, and thou shalt be the tail. Deuteronomy 28:44

Poverty is a by-product of transgressing God's law and walking in sin. If it is not you in particular, it could be generations past.

Thou shalt not bow down thyself to them, nor serve them: for I the LORD thy God am a jealous God, visiting the iniquity of the fathers upon the children unto the third and fourth generation of them that hate me; Exodus 20:5

Poverty is a tool in the hand of the devil for execution or destruction of people.

The rich man's wealth is his strong city: the destruction of the poor is their poverty. Proverbs 10:15

Poverty is producing the wealth of the nations for the rich to enjoy.

The rich ruleth over the poor, and the borrower is servant to the lender. Proverbs 22:7

In almost every economy, the rich truly rule over the poor. The rich work for lesser time and for better pay, while the poor man's labour is harder and his compensation is lesser.

Poverty is having no choice and having to make do with leftovers, second-hand and rejected things.

And thou shalt not glean thy vineyard, neither shalt thou gather every grape of thy vineyard; thou shalt leave them for the poor and stranger: I am the LORD your God. Leviticus 19:10

When thou gatherest the grapes of thy vineyard, thou shalt not glean it afterward: it shall be for the stranger, for the fatherless, and for the widow. Deuteronomy 24:21

And when ye reap the harvest of your land, thou shalt not make clean riddance of the corners of thy field when thou reapest, neither shalt thou gather any gleaning of thy harvest: thou shalt leave them unto the poor, and to the stranger: I am the LORD your God. Leviticus 23:22

Poverty is having no choice as to where you live. It is allowing others to determine the economy, your residency and your location in life.

Wealth maketh many friends; but the poor is separated from his neighbour. Proverbs 19:4

Poverty means you are being despised by your friends and rejected by them.

All the brethren of the poor do hate him: how much more do his friends go far from him? He pursueth them with words, yet they are wanting to him. Proverbs 19:7

Poverty puts a man under the perpetual rule of the rich.

The rich determine your voice, your location, your life, your future and your clothes.

The rich ruleth over the poor, and the borrower is servant to the lender. Proverbs 22:7

Sometimes it is hard to assimilate these, but imagine the poor man who rents the house built by the rich. He has to think first of his house rent before he can clothe his family.

The economy determines the movement, joy and pace of the family of a poor man. He is unable to take his destiny in his own hands.

Poverty is when others have to always be your spokesperson.

The rich are in the habit of making themselves the spokesperson for the poor.

A feast is made for laughter, and wine maketh merry: but money answereth all things. Ecclesiastes 10:19

Poverty means somebody else taking the credit for all the hard work you have done.

In any organisation the poor are never remembered for the hard work they have done, but rather those who played a lesser role. Those who own the place are the ones who are attributed to be very successful and hard working.

Poverty is rooted in a curse and therefore things seem to fall through every time you are about to breakthrough.

> *The impotent man answered him, Sir, I have no man, when the water is troubled, to put me into the pool: but while I am coming, another steppeth down before me. John 5:7*

When you are fighting a poverty spirit you can barely make ends meet and have difficulty enjoying a decent life. The spirit of poverty may be present when you observe that every hard work and endeavour that you carry out is met with frustration and a shortage of financial supply.

Hard work and a little supply is a sign that the spirit of poverty is manifest.

One of the greatest challenges of poverty is that when the spirit of poverty rules over a man's life, he will be doing things he does not like, working in a place he does not like, earning a salary he does not like, working with people he does not like.

A poverty spirit may be around if your income does not match with your ever expanding needs.

Failure and poverty take away the right of such people to speak of success. Failure and poverty give the impression that you are not a hard worker when as a matter of fact, you are a harder worker, but with a poorer proof.

A poverty spirit makes people sometimes resist a teaching that will help them to break free from the cycle of lack that they are facing and therefore perpetuating their bondage in the chain and captivity of lack. The spirit of poverty has a strong mind and it wants to stay as long as the man who is entrapped would permit. Because a man is educated does not guarantee prosperity. The spirit has to be dealt with and the mindset has to change.

The mindset of poverty brings along with it sickness, disease and other challenges.

Where there is poverty, sorrow robs the home of joy and releases perpetual arguments.

The presence of poverty gives rise to difficulties, fights, and arguments within the family and among friends.

This does not mean in effect that the rich do not argue or the wealthy do not argue. As a matter of fact, wealth without a purpose can be a reason for perpetual argument.

Better is a dry morsel, and quietness therewith, than an house full of sacrifices with strife. Proverbs 17:1

Poverty stays perpetually when one tries to justify his present location in life.

Poverty will stay perpetually if one is critical of those who teach and believe that Christians should prosper.

The spirit of poverty will make a person believe that others, including ministers of God do not deserve to experience the prosperity of God.

That must be the reason why Judas reacted at the woman who broke the alabaster box. Judas is a representative of people who have a poverty spirit and tend to compete with the blessed. The poor do not want to pay the price it takes to come out of the cycle in which they have found themselves. Sometimes they have a mindset that if they do not give but if they are committed to living right, they might just prosper.

When a man is controlled by a poverty mindset, even if he was led by the Spirit of God to give, he resists it. The mindset of the poor makes it hard for him to trust in God's ability to break him free from his cycle of lack. The mindset of the poor makes him to be governed more by fear than by faith. The poor person often has money fears rather than faith and confidence that things will change. One might ask,

WHAT IS AT THE ROOT OF THE MINDSET OF THE POOR?

1.Laziness

The slothful man roasteth not that which he took in hunting: but the substance of a diligent man is precious. Proverbs 12:27

Laziness is a major cause of poverty; the inability to give all it takes to break from a cycle. Laziness is not only a matter of physical laziness, it could be mental, spiritual or emotional. The man who is mentally lazy will not pay the price it takes to re-educate himself and therefore increase his cycle of income. For example, if a 40 year old who only has primary school level education decides to educate himself, it will only take 13 years to have a doctorate degree in any chosen field.

2. Drunkenness and gluttony

Drunkenness and gluttony are major causes of poverty in several economies. Sometimes actions are taken that deliberately keep some people in a state of drunkenness. Around the mines of South Africa, the miners who spend all their life digging the gold also spend all their evenings spending their earnings on the beer parlours and the houses of prostitutes around the mines. The cycle continues until they are either old or laid off and the same is replicated in many other economies.

Some poor people are also in the habit of blaming their destiny on fate so that while they struggle with bouts of inferiority, their possibilities become limitations. There is a refusal to confront the truth as to the cause of poverty. For those who are born again, biblical ignorance is a major reason for poverty, particularly where certain church cultures and belief systems have been absorbed and elevated above scripture.

Misquoting scripture and the misuse of scripture can cause poverty.

For example, people will quote the scripture and say, "Godliness and contentment is great gain" but they quote it as if it means, "Godliness and containment".

But godliness with contentment is great gain.1 Timothy 6:6

The Bible does not make godliness synonymous with poverty, rather it says, "A righteous man leaves an inheritance for his children's children". Abraham was blessed and the scriptures say that Levi paid the tithe in Abraham, which means that whatever Abraham had was for four generations.

Contentment means to have satisfaction, to know fulfilment, to have joy and to have pleasure in life. If that is absent, then it is containment. Great gain on the other hand means huge profit, abundance and plenty. Therefore to use it to justify lack would be a malapropism. Another scripture often misquoted is when people say, "Money is the root of all evil". The scripture renders it differently.

For the love of money is the root of all evil: which while some coveted after, they have erred from the faith, and pierced themselves through with many sorrows. 1 Timothy 6:10

If there is any scripture people would use often times to argue that rich people will never go to heaven, it would be the story of Lazarus, as it is often used to justify lack as a way of expressing holiness. It is a misuse of scripture because Abraham who also featured in the story of Lazarus was said to be rich.

And Abram was very rich in cattle, in silver, and in gold. Genesis 13:2

Lazarus made it to heaven. The only thing he missed out on was his blessing on earth. Abraham was blessed both on earth and in heaven.

Poor people blame a lack of contacts for their state of being.

The impotent man answered him, Sir, I have no man, when the water is troubled, to put me into the pool: but while I am coming, another steppeth down before me. John 5:7

He used his condition to justify his limitations. However, the scripture makes us understand abundantly that God is a very present help in the time of need.

God is our refuge and strength, a very present help in trouble. Psalm 46:1

3.The lack of education

Another major source of justification for poverty for many people is the lack of education. Education cannot be an excuse because we have already said earlier that even a 40 year old with a primary school leaving certificate can have a doctorate degree by the time they are 53 if they set their mind to it. However, a greater percentage of the wealthy of the world did not become so because of education, but because they set their mind and committed themselves to one thing.

Imagine therefore the believer who along with setting their mind to one thing also has Christ. Balloons do not rise because of their colour but their content.

Poverty may be a product of despising blessed people.

You never rise to what you despise. You never inspect what you do not respect.

Poverty is a product of a wrong belief that being poor stands for righteousness.

There are many who even in their lack have carried out righteous acts. If there is anything that ties the poor to the bondage of lack, it is sometimes the belief that God has ordained it to be so. Also, by misquoting the scripture that says, "The poor and the rich, the Lord God made them," many miss the word in that verse which says, "The Lord God made them both," not "The Lord God made them so."

The rich and poor meet together: the LORD is the maker of them all. Proverbs 22:2

God is no respecter of persons, He gives power to get wealth, not only to the wealthy. His desire is your prosperity as long as it will be used for the advancement of His kingdom and the well being of your family.

THE CURE

Is there a cure for the mindset of the poor? The answer certainly is yes. However, the first act must be to make up your mind to break free from the spirit of poverty.

> *And Jabez was more honourable than his brethren: and his mother called his name Jabez, saying, Because I bare him with sorrow. And Jabez called on the God of Israel, saying, Oh that thou wouldest bless me indeed, and enlarge my coast, and that thine hand might be with me, and that thou wouldest keep me from evil, that it may not grieve me! And God granted him that which he requested. 1 Chronicles 4:9-10*

To eradicate poverty you must be ready to reject the traditions of men.

One of the last Goliaths to fall before believers is the Goliath of financial need and Goliath always justifies his right to hold you down, attack you and keep you in lack. For many believers, the reason for poverty is that they have not dealt with their money fears. All humans, one way or the other have money fears.

Eradication of poverty requires that you unlearn every wrong belief from previous church backgrounds and stereotypes you have heard.

Many times we do not know how poverty has influenced our thoughts. Take yourself through a simple test. You go to a restaurant and you are given the menu. Where do you look, the left or the right? If you look to the right, you are concerned about the price, if you look to the left, you are concerned about the quality. Cheap is not always the best, neither does opulence mean you are a good money manager.

The scriptures say a poor man is hated by his neighbours. Why is it so? Probably because he does not know how to bless others or the quality of the atmosphere and place he is able to live in is also where poverty makes people act wrong.

Wealth maketh many friends; but the poor is separated from his neighbour. Proverbs 19:4

All the brethren of the poor do hate him: how much more do his friends go far from him? He pursueth them with words, yet they are wanting to him. Proverbs 19:7

Rejection follows where there is poverty. Therefore find the scriptures that challenge you to live a life of victory and that which is positive. Intelligence is not enough. Intelligent people are sometimes poor therefore it is important to know the Lord in order to break free from the cycle of poverty. Poverty may be a by-product of a three or four generational curse. Remember the scriptures and only hold on to the scriptures until you have your deliverance.

Christ hath redeemed us from the curse of the law, being made a curse for us: for it is written, Cursed is every one that hangeth on a tree: That the blessing of Abraham might come on the Gentiles through Jesus Christ; that we might receive the promise of the Spirit through faith. Galatians 3:13-14

Poverty is a reason why many compromise their position.

Poverty is the most major reason for prostitution, drug use, burglary and stealing.

Poverty is the reason for corruption in nations.

It is hard to bribe a policeman who is adequately paid.

Some depressions and mental illnesses have poverty at their root.

Therefore you must make up your mind to know the blessing of the Lord. Many people cannot cope when poverty hits, sometimes it takes them to the point of suicide. You must clearly establish in your mind that poverty is not from God. God made all things richly for us to enjoy.

> *Charge them that are rich in this world, that they be not highminded, nor trust in uncertain riches, but in the living God, who giveth us richly all things to enjoy; 1 Timothy 6:17*

> *To an inheritance incorruptible, and undefiled, and that fadeth not away, reserved in heaven for you, 1 Peter 1:4*

So, until the mindset is corrected, your pocket has been set. A poverty mindset affects your giving to God and your giving to man. A poverty mindset is behind hoarding and the refusal to bless others.

-3-
THE MOTIVES

Money is a neutral instrument of exchange used by all societies from when it was introduced in early Mesopotamia. The neutrality of money therefore means that money has no enemy, neither has it its own character. Money assumes the character of the owner. In the hand of the philanthropist it builds hospitals, homes, orphanages and brings hope to the hopeless. In the hand of the drug addict it destroys life. In the hand of the God-loving believer, it builds things that make up the kingdom of God, advancing the gospel and helping unreached people to be reached. Money in the hand of a destroyer would mean the acquisition of weapons of destruction. Money indeed is a neutral instrument.

There is always a motive behind people's desire to have money; whether spoken or unspoken. This motive underwrites a person's pursuit or lack of zeal. From a biblical point of view, it can be said that there are positive reasons for wanting to be blessed financially and there are negative reasons.

a. POSITIVE MOTIVATION

1. Personal comfort and convenience

No matter how people extol the virtues of lack, no matter how humbled we are at the sight of people who survive in the midst of extreme lack and poverty, the innate desire is still to have our needs met, to experience a certain degree of comfort and convenience in life.

2. Family comfort and convenience

But if any provide not for his own, and specially for those of his own house, he hath denied the faith, and is worse than an infidel. 1 Timothy 5:8

One of the cardinal duties of the head of any household is to be the provider. From Adam to the caveman, from the caveman to the jet-age man, that role has not changed. There is still the understanding that someone has to provide for the convenience of their family. The degree of convenience that we provide for our family is often such that we desire it to be better than what we experienced with our own parents.

The scriptures also teach that it is one who not only provides but preserves for his grandchildren that is truly a blessed man. That desire to see our children and grandchildren live and have a better life increases our motivation.

A good man leaveth an inheritance to his children's children: and the wealth of the sinner is laid up for the just. Proverbs 13:22

3. As a tool of ministry

And God is able to make all grace abound toward you; that ye, always having all sufficiency in all things, may abound to every good work. 2 Corinthians 9:8

Therefore, as ye abound in every thing, in faith, and utterance, and knowledge, and in all diligence, and in your love to us, see that ye abound in this grace also. I speak not by commandment, but by occasion of the forwardness of others, and to prove the sincerity of your love. 2 Corinthians 8:7-8

The gospel needs to be spread around the world and it is clear and obvious that the unsaved would rather spend their money saving the endangered species of the Amazon jungle, than use it to sponsor the gospel of Jesus Christ. The church has sometimes succumbed to the fear of criticism and therefore refused to play its role in challenging the people of God to give.

How then shall they call on him in whom they have not believed? and how shall they believe in him of whom they have not heard? and how shall they hear without a preacher? And how shall they preach, except they be sent? as it is written, How beautiful are the feet of them that preach the gospel of peace, and bring glad tidings of good things! But they have not all obeyed the gospel. For Esaias saith, Lord, who hath believed our report? So then faith cometh by hearing, and hearing by the word of God. Romans 10:14-17

People cannot hear without the preacher being sent and the preacher cannot go without enough financial backing.

No one can march on an empty stomach.

4. It is God's will that Christians be financially empowered

But thou shalt remember the LORD thy God: for it is he that giveth thee power to get wealth, that he may establish his covenant which he sware unto thy fathers, as it is this day. Deuteronomy 8:18

The understanding that financial blessing glorifies God in the life of the Christian becomes a strong source of motivation.

It is the blessing of the Lord that makes rich and adds no sorrow:

Beloved, I wish above all things that thou mayest prosper and be in health, even as thy soul prospereth. 3 John 2

5. Blessed to be a blessing

That they do good, that they be rich in good works, ready to distribute, willing to communicate. 1 Timothy 6:18

And I will make of thee a great nation, and I will bless thee, and make thy name great; and thou shalt be a blessing. Genesis 12:2

The word blessing means to be empowered. When you are empowered financially or with blessing, what the scriptures mean in effect is that you are a distribution centre. People's ability to distribute what God brings into their life determines how much of it they come into. The kingdom of God is not for hoarders. In effect one of the greatest motivations is the desire to be blessed in order to bless others.

6. Money is a defence

If you check your wallet you probably have some money or credit cards. We do not realise how much the need to carry money has influenced our society. The more people have, the more secure they feel financially. I consider this to be a positive motivation as long as having money does not make money have you.

For wisdom is a defence, and money is a defence: but the excellency of knowledge is, that wisdom giveth life to them that have it. Ecclesiastes 7:12

7. A sense of security

The future cannot be predicted and even if you say you know how to manage yourself and bring control into what you do, nature, circumstances and the intrusion of other people can change your world. It is in the light of this that people take on insurance. Medical, automobile, housing, house contents insurance, life insurance etc.

Money becomes a defence when it brings a sense of security when people have taken care of these areas. A person who takes on life insurance seems to have a sense of comfort that their loved ones would not suffer financially at their departure. Other forms of financial security that we put in place are in the form of savings, investments and involvement in pension schemes.

8. Ministering to the household of faith

As we have therefore opportunity, let us do good unto all men, especially unto them who are of the household of faith. Galatians 6:12

The scripture encourages us to not only be believers in word but in deed. We must be a blessing to the fallen, the faltering, the far and the faithful. It is interesting then whatever becomes common is forgotten. There are always people around you to whom you can minister. It is not uncommon in certain churches for individuals to feel that God has spoken to them to bless people financially.

9. Kingdom promotion

This gospel shall be preached in all the world and then the end shall come.

The preaching of the gospel to all the world was a task that looked almost impossible. In today's world of the satellite communication system, nothing seems impossible. You can communicate simultaneously through linking various satellites to almost all of the world. These things would only be possible as Christians come into their wealthy place.

Thou hast caused men to ride over our heads; we went through fire and through water: but thou broughtest us out into a wealthy place. Psalm 66:12

b. NEGATIVE MOTIVATION

1. When money becomes an object of devotion or worship

No man can serve two masters: for either he will hate the one, and love the other; or else he will hold to the one, and despise the other. Ye cannot serve God and mammon. Matthew 6:24

Jesus' statement suggests the fact that the degree of commitment people are ready to give to make money could make it an object of devotion and worship. Once our pursuit has been corrupted by a desire that is almost uncontrollable, it influences the time people have for things other than making money. They sleep, dream, eat and meditate money. Devotion to money is not only the problem of the wealthy, it could be the challenge of the 'have nots' because money seems to elude them.

Worshippers of mammon do it also because they believe that once you have money, the world bows to you.

2. People pressure

People pressure could be wanting to keep up with the Joneses, the demand people put on us to make money or the bombardment of our mind by the degree of advertising for a certain kind of luxury and lifestyle.

3. Envy

But as for me, my feet were almost gone; my steps had well nigh slipped. For I was envious at the foolish, when I saw the prosperity of the wicked. Psalm 73:2-3

Asaph the worship leader in the temple in the days of David was carried away by envy because of the prosperity of the wicked. Envy will make a man covet what the financially blessed have. Envy will make a man pursue what the financially blessed have. The envious think that life is comfortable for the wealthy, and everything seems to work, and therefore the envious would prefer the life of the wealthy, because all they see is the physical comfort and may not know other awaiting challenges.

4. For personal validation

Have you ever had a parcel delivered by one of the major courier companies and when you received it, it was damaged on delivery? Well that seems to be the experience of almost all humans. Whether we were raised in homes of great luxury and comfort or in the most dejected troublous settings, a certain degree of damage was left on us. This in effect affects our self-esteem and confidence. At the root of some people's motive for seeking for money is in order to prop their sense of value and acceptance.

Money may truly bring status, however sociologists argue that it cannot give you class. The irony of it also is that you can have class without money.

5. Hoarding

Close to seeking money for personal validation is hoarding. At the root of hoarding are two things. The first is our money fears. People often hoard because they are afraid they might go back to the poverty they once knew. Unless a man educates his mind, the characteristics of people who once knew extreme poverty and later knew great wealth is the challenge of knowing if they should spend at all. They hoard because they do not want to go back to the day when they slept on the street or went to bed on an empty stomach.

The other reason is for boosting their self-esteem. When money becomes your source of boosting your self-esteem, it comes into every conversation as a proof of your right to belong, to speak and to act.

6. Money for the game of it

There are men who are very wealthy and have no need for extra money, but the pursuit of it has become a game. Their motive for having more is not to meet a need, touch a life, promote the kingdom of God, help their family, but for the game of it; the ability to show conquest of the one thing that seems to elude the majority of the people of the world.

7. Loving it

For the love of money is the root of all evil: which while some coveted after, they have erred from the faith, and pierced themselves through with many sorrows. 1 Timothy 6:10

The Webster's Dictionary gives synonyms of love as: affection, attachment, attraction, charity, devotion, esteem, feeling, fondness, friendship, liking, passion, regard, tenderness.

In the sense of affection it means to be 'with kindly feeling, deep, tender, constant, going out to some person or object.'

Love is the yearning or outgoing of the soul towards something that is regarded as excellent, beautiful or desirable. It is a strong and absorbing affection or an attraction towards a person or an object. It is more intense, absorbing and tender than friendship. More intense, impulsive and passionate than affection. Once that becomes a description of a person's attitude to money, money has become central and the motive for having it has now made money to be a deity, and the worship can only best be described as mammonism.

One of the key problems at the root of the debate on prosperity within the church is the motive of pursuit. People with good intentions have found their minds corrupted in the past. So good intention is not enough as the reason for the pursuit of prosperity. It is important not only to know positive motives, but also to know how to keep your heart pure and right before and after you have been blessed.

1. Have a heart of purity

It is righteousness that triggers the blessing of God.

Say ye to the righteous, that it shall be well with him: for they shall eat the fruit of their doings. Isaiah 3:10

Once your heart is wrong you can be excluded from the blessing belonging to you. A good example of this is Adam; he was stripped of the glory, favour and blessing that was his because he walked in disobedience.

And when the woman saw that the tree was good for food, and that it was pleasant to the eyes, and a tree to be desired to make one wise, she took of the fruit thereof, and did eat, and gave also unto her husband with her; and he did eat. And the eyes of them both were opened, and they knew that they were naked; and they sewed fig leaves together, and made themselves aprons. Genesis 3:6-7

Israel was brought out of Egypt but they were given the answer to reaching Canaan land and enjoying the blessing of Canaan.

If ye be willing and obedient, ye shall eat the good of the land: Isaiah 1:19

Canaan land, the place of God's blessing is where you should be.

Thou hast caused men to ride over our heads; we went through fire and through water: but thou broughtest us out into a wealthy place. Psalm 66:12

Psalm 66:12 is the wealthy place, but there are people who are excluded from there. You do not want to be outside, because the Bible says, those who are kept outside are dogs.

For without are dogs, and sorcerers, and whoremongers, and murderers, and idolaters, and whosoever loveth and maketh a lie. Revelation 22:15

Once God's Word becomes your delight and keeps your heart pure, it is impossible for you to resist the blessings of God.

And he shall be like a tree planted by the rivers of water, that bringeth forth his fruit in his season; his leaf also shall not wither; and whatsoever he doeth shall prosper. Psalm 1:3

Riches and honour are with me; yea, durable riches and righteousness. Proverbs 8:18

Purity aligns you in readiness for the profit of God that will follow. It does not automatically bring everything you need. You must also know how to run your vision.

For bodily exercise profiteth little: but godliness is profitable unto all things, having promise of the life that now is, and of that which is to come. 1 Timothy 4:8

2. Have implicit trust in God

When others trust in the chariots of commerce and personal ability, your motives will be kept right if your trust continuously rests in God.

Some trust in chariots, and some in horses: but we will remember the name of the LORD our God. Psalm 20:7

How easy it is for one to trust in the things provided, but you must keep your eyes on the Lord.

I will lift up mine eyes unto the hills, from whence cometh my help. Psalm 121:1

Your knowledge, ability, association, ingenuity or strength is not enough. It is God who prospers those who trust in Him.

Trust in the LORD with all thine heart; and lean not unto thine own understanding. In all thy ways acknowledge him, and he shall direct thy paths. Proverbs 3:5-6

Trust is proof that you know the source of your blessing. Your continuous emphasis on the trust of God is what will put a difference between mere abundant money and the prosperity of God. Your trust in God is one thing you will hold on to so that when the blessing comes, your mind does not drift to think that it was a connection, or the ability of man or the strength of your vision but rather a door opened by God.

3. Be a distribution centre

And I will make of thee a great nation, and I will bless thee, and make thy name great; and thou shalt be a blessing: Genesis 12:2

Your desire to have must be accompanied by a desire to release. Giving is living, releasing is increasing. Sowing causes reaping. God desires to give, but He chooses to whom He does. He gives to those who have the ability to give it away. He gave Joseph such abundance, because of all the 12 sons of Jacob he had a more magnanimous heart to forgive the others. Imagine if it was Simeon or Judah that was promoted in Egypt; they probably would have gone after the other 11 brothers.

Satan robs, God gives and because we are God's children, let us show the proof of whose offspring we are.

4. Be committed to doing good

This makes your motive right and makes the blessing flow.

That they do good, that they be rich in good works, ready to distribute, willing to communicate; 1 Timothy 6:18

Our motive must be to touch the household of God. We must sow into the life of those who cannot give it back to us.

And let us not be weary in well doing: for in due season we shall reap, if we faint not. Galatians 6:9

When we do this, we lend to God.

He that hath pity upon the poor lendeth unto the LORD; and that which he hath given will he pay him again. Proverbs 19:17

Such acts continually make seed to be in your hand so that you continue to distribute to the members of the household who need to know the grace of God.

5. Recognise God's commitment to you

If ye be willing and obedient, ye shall eat the good of the land: Isaiah 1:19

If they obey and serve him, they shall spend their days in prosperity, and their years in pleasures. Job 36:11

6. Recognise that the wealth of God is looking for covenant people who have the anointing to handle it

Unlike the man who is negatively motivated to pursue wealth, Christians are one unusual group of people whom wealth is looking for to rest upon. Fools are destroyed by their own prosperity, but the righteous man will abound with good things. God will cause the grace, anointing and ability to handle the coming blessing to come upon you first and then He will release the blessing. Once motives are right, the blessings will come.

-4-
THE MANDATE

In 3 John chapter 1 verse 2 the wish of God is expressed.

Beloved, I wish above all things that thou mayest prosper and be in health, even as thy soul prospereth. 3 John 1:2

With this in mind it means in effect that God's plan is for the blessing of the believer. However, if the blessing of God is eluding you, there must be a reason. Because having come into the knowledge of salvation through Christ, everything God has is now made available to you.

According as his divine power hath given unto us all things that pertain unto life and godliness, through the knowledge of him that hath called us to glory and virtue: 2 Peter 1:3

There is always a reason for the absence of supply, there is a cause for every effect. That cause and effect is what underwrites the   principle or the law of sowing and reaping.

While the earth remaineth, seedtime and harvest, and cold and heat, and summer and winter, and day and night shall not cease. Genesis 8:22

If you can get to the root cause of the lack you are experiencing, then you can be released into God's original intention for your blessing. The result in effect will be wealth. God's plan is for the blessing of Abraham to rest on us.

Christ hath redeemed us from the curse of the law, being made a curse for us: for it is written, Cursed is every one that hangeth on a tree: That the blessing of Abraham might come on the Gentiles through Jesus Christ; that we might receive the promise of the Spirit through faith. Galatians 3:13-14

That blessing includes the promise of the Spirit of God by faith. It also includes the fullness of the presence of the Holy Spirit and His flow in the presence of the life of a believer. It is also having everything God promised in His covenant with Abraham. Remember God promised to bless Abraham.

Now the LORD had said unto Abram, Get thee out of thy country, and from thy kindred, and from thy father's house, unto a land that I will shew thee: And I will make of thee a great nation, and I will bless thee, and make thy name great; and thou shalt be a blessing: And I will bless them that bless thee, and curse him that curseth thee: and in thee shall all families of the earth be blessed. Genesis 12:1-3

It is a promise of having the enemy smitten before your face and dispersed according to God's Word. That enemy includes financial adversity. However if this is the mandate, then the question is, is this the experience of most believers? Are you finding fulfilment in what you are doing? Are you blossoming and expressing the gift of God planted in you? Are you achieving all that God has given you the ability to achieve? Do you sense growth in your personal life and dream? Are you reaping harvests in the field God has planted for you?

God's plan is sometimes contrary to what we are experiencing. His plan is to supply our need according to His riches in glory. The season is not as far as we think.

> *If the clouds be full of rain, they empty themselves upon the earth: and if the tree fall toward the south, or toward the north, in the place where the tree falleth, there it shall be. He that observeth the wind shall not sow; and he that regardeth the clouds shall not reap. As thou knowest not what is the way of the spirit, nor how the bones do grow in the womb of her that is with child: even so thou knowest not the works of God who maketh all. In the morning sow thy seed, and in the evening withhold not thine hand: for thou knowest not whether shall prosper, either this or that, or whether they both shall be alike good. Eccl.11:3-6*

God's harvest is a ready one and He wants to bring it into our lives immediately. Until you search diligently you may not recognise the harvest God already has for you.

> *Say not ye, There are yet four months, and then cometh harvest? behold, I say unto you, Lift up your eyes, and look on the fields; for they are white already to harvest. John 4:35*

Until you engage yourself in your field, there will be no wages. Fruitfulness follows finding the appropriate field and being diligent in that field.

> *And he that reapeth receiveth wages, and gathereth fruit unto life eternal: that both he that soweth and he that reapeth may rejoice together. John 4:36*

Your breakthrough in life is in your field, not what works for somebody else. Your actualisation is tied to the discovery of the field of your dreams. Jesus said, "Lift up your eyes and look."

Say not ye, There are yet four months, and then cometh harvest? behold, I say unto you, Lift up your eyes, and look on the fields; for they are white already to harvest. John 4:35

Until you find your field of dreams, happiness eludes you, the struggle continues and life is a continuous fight. The mandate for financial blessing is certainly that there is a divine field ready for your harvest. It is a matured harvest field waiting for you to put in the sickle. You must be ready to see that harvest with the eyes of God.

For the seed shall be prosperous; the vine shall give her fruit, and the ground shall give her increase, and the heavens shall give their dew; and I will cause the remnant of this people to possess all these things. Zechariah 8:12

Your chief quest is to know where God has planted His harvest for you. If you have the field of God's planting you will have the blessing of Deuteronomy 28, not the curses. So I ask you again, is your present work the most fulfilling you could do?

WORKING IN A CURSED FIELD

If you are not in the field God has planted for you, if you are in a cursed field you cannot experience the favour God marked you out for. There is a handful of purpose marked out with your name on it, but it can only be yours if you can search for it. It can only be yours if you find it.

And let fall also some of the handfuls of purpose for her, and leave them, that she may glean them, and rebuke her not. Ruth 2:16

There shall be an handful of corn in the earth upon the top of the mountains; the fruit thereof shall shake like Lebanon: and they of the city shall flourish like grass of the earth. Psalm 72:16

Better is an handful with quietness, than both the hands full with travail and vexation of spirit. Ecclesiastes 4:6

You might be tilling a cursed field when you violate the laws in Deuteronomy 28 that requires obedience to God's voice.

But it shall come to pass, if thou wilt not hearken unto the voice of the LORD thy God, to observe to do all his commandments and his statutes which I command thee this day; that all these curses shall come upon thee, and overtake thee: Cursed shalt thou be in the city, and cursed shalt thou be in the field. Cursed shall be thy basket and thy store. Deuteronomy 28:15-17

So in spite of the mandate to be blessed, your work either reflects a blessing or the curse of God. We see in the case of Adam that his mandate changed because his work was now cursed.

And unto Adam he said, Because thou hast hearkened unto the voice of thy wife, and hast eaten of the tree, of which I commanded thee, saying, Thou shalt not eat of it: cursed is the ground for thy sake; in sorrow shalt thou eat of it all the days of thy life; Thorns also and thistles shall it bring forth to thee; and thou shalt eat the herb of the field; In the sweat of thy face shalt thou eat bread, till thou return unto the ground; for out of it wast thou taken: for dust thou art, and unto dust shalt thou return. Genesis 3:17-19

How do you know if you are outside of your mandate? Do you have a vision, but for some years something has held you back, preventing you from marching towards its fulfilment? You may be out of your mandate. If you have felt a strangling or stifling of your dream, you may be out of your mandate. There is probably something you are overlooking that is connected to a cursed field.

HARVESTING THE FIELD OF GOD'S PLANTING

Operating within the mandate of God for your financial blessing therefore means to find a field God has planted you in and harvest it. Genesis 1:28 gives us a breakdown of God's mandate.

And God blessed them, and God said unto them, Be fruitful, and multiply, and replenish the earth, and subdue it: and have dominion over the fish of the sea, and over the fowl of the air, and over every living thing that moveth upon the earth. Genesis 1:28

Firstly it says to bear fruit.

This implies enjoying perpetual harvests. Being fruitful is the process of bringing fruit to maturity. In other words the mandate of God is to see that when you lay your hands on things, you should experience financial blessing to its fullness. It is to produce more seed from harvests to create perpetual harvests. Not just getting a job, but working to perpetuate your financial harvest. So it is not enough to bear fruit, it is important that you create a seed atmosphere for continuous fruitfulness in your finances. Blessing was intended by God to be perpetuated.

The second word in this verse is to multiply.

This is to increase anything by duplicating it. God

designed us to duplicate or to raise a standard around us. To multiply means no matter what field of business you may enter, there is almost no original idea anymore, but you can raise the standard above how you met it.

The third word is to replenish.

This means to constantly supply and refill whatever becomes depleted. The mandate for financial blessing on the believer is not to replicate what he sees other people do with money or have the same attitude. Instead of complaining about what is not working, we were designed to fill the gap with new and creative ideas from God. If you do not like what you see in society, fill it up again. If you do not like the brokenness in the life of some people, fix the problem. If you do not like the demise of the morality around you, fix it. If you do not like the loneliness of the elderly, find a solution. If you do not like the pain children are going through find an answer. Have compassion for young mothers who have no answer to their predicament. To replenish is to give money a mission. Look for abandoned, abused and hurt children and minister to them; that is money with a mandate.

The fourth word in this verse is to subdue.

This means to bring all chaotic, lawless, aimless obstacles in subjection to your purpose by conquering them. No matter how you feel about yourself, God gave you the gift of subduing. That is why He ordained you a champion and a conqueror when you were even   little in your own eyes.

Nay, in all these things we are more than conquerors through him that loved us. Romans 8:37

To subdue is to enter the wealthy place God designed you for. The place of fruit bearing, multiplication, replenishing, subduing and dominion. When you understand the mandate you carry, then it is time for you to enter and harvest the field that has your name on it.

The last word in the verse is dominion.

The person who would experience financial blessing, the believer who will walk in the fullness of God's prosperity must not be a push over, a quitter or a person who wants to walk away from challenges. Such a person must place his faith and trust in God. Understanding your mandate should provoke a vision for life. When that takes place, provision will follow. God releases provision where there is a vision.

Three things often motivate people; need, greed or vision. Some have great needs; they strive for wealth, believing it will satisfy their emptiness. Others simply desire to be rich because they have a certain greed and lust after material things. A lustful motivation to gain wealth drives the man who has need or the one who is driven by greed. When your quest to carry out the mandate of blessing is rooted in vision, the wealth that comes from it would not control you but help the fulfilment of your dream.

The wealth God has and wants to pour out far surpasses your current need. The presence of need is not enough motivation for receiving what God has. Wealth only follows when there is a God-given vision. God adds everything you want, when you seek Him.

But seek ye first the kingdom of God, and his righteousness; and all these things shall be added unto you. Matthew 6:33

Israel had a vision of reaching the Promised Land; that vision caused a provision. For 40 years in the wilderness the heavens opened and manna rained upon God's people.

Abraham was under a mandate to be a blessing to the world and for believing God enough, God made it happen.

Now the LORD had said unto Abram, Get thee out of thy country, and from thy kindred, and from thy father's house, unto a land that I will shew thee:And I will make of thee a great nation, and I will bless thee, and make thy name great; and thou shalt be a blessing:And I will bless them that bless thee, and curse him that curseth thee: and in thee shall all families of the earth be blessed. Genesis 12:1-3

By reason of a mandate, God committed to supernaturally provide all that Abraham would need to make that vision possible.

And the LORD said unto Abram, after that Lot was separated from him, Lift up now thine eyes, and look from the place where thou art northward, and southward, and eastward, and westward: For all the land which thou seest, to thee will I give it, and to thy seed for ever. And I will make thy seed as the dust of the earth: so that if a man can number the dust of the earth, then shall thy seed also be numbered. Arise, walk through the land in the length of it and in the breadth of it; for I will give it unto thee. Genesis 13:14-17

Once you understand the mandate of God, circumstances do not control you. With the departure of Abraham it is safe to conclude that maybe he did not leave any wealth for Isaac to use, however Isaac knew that once there was a mandate, there will be a supply. He acted in faith and experienced God's promise.

Then Isaac sowed in that land, and received in the same year an hundredfold: and the LORD blessed him. And the man waxed great, and went forward, and grew until he became very great: for he had possession of flocks, and possession of herds, and great store of servants: and the Philistines envied him. Genesis 26:12-14

Jacob the carrier of the patriarchal covenant also understood that there may be delay, but God's promise could not be denied.

And he dreamed, and behold a ladder set up on the earth, and the top of it reached to heaven: and behold the angels of God ascending and descending on it. And, behold, the LORD stood above it, and said, I am the LORD God of Abraham thy father, and the God of Isaac: the land whereon thou liest, to thee will I give it, and to thy seed; And thy seed shall be as the dust of the earth, and thou shalt spread abroad to the west, and to the east, and to the north, and to the south: and in thee and in thy seed shall all the families of the earth be blessed. Genesis 28:12-14

So a mandate cannot be erased by delay or battles, even if you have to wait for it just know it will come to pass. Jacob had to wait for 20 years for the fulfilment of God's financial mandate upon his life.

And he said, What shall I give thee? And Jacob said, Thou shalt not give me any thing: if thou wilt do this thing for me, I will again feed and keep thy flock: Genesis 30:31

... though it tarry, wait for it; because it will surely come, it will not tarry. Habakkuk 2:3

The understanding that there is a mandate for your financial blessing should make you know that the wealth of God is looking for those who can handle it. When you walk under the mandate, God will make you experience the days of heaven on earth.

That your days may be multiplied, and the days of your children, in the land which the LORD sware unto your fathers to give them, as the days of heaven upon the earth. Deuteronomy 11:21

When you walk under the mandate you will be ready to stop working so hard to make things happen, you will be ready to stop hitch-hiking on the highway of life, you will be ready to enter your own wealthy place. You will be ready to know the joy of giving and receiving what God has for you.

WHAT KIND OF FINANCIAL BLESSING DOES THIS MANDATE ENTAIL?

1. Spiritual prosperity

And this is life eternal, that they might know thee the only true God, and Jesus Christ, whom thou hast sent. John 17:3

And be not drunk with wine, wherein is excess; but be filled with the Spirit; Ephesians 5:18

Everything hinges on your soul prospering, because if you are deficient spiritually you will not be able to enjoy your financial mandate.

Beloved, I wish above all things that thou mayest prosper and be in health, even as thy soul prospereth. 3 John 1:2

2. Mental prosperity

A sound mind is required to manage the level of financial favour that God wants to bring to the life of the believer.

For God hath not given us the spirit of fear; but of power, and of love, and of a sound mind. 2 Timothy 1:7

Thou wilt keep him in perfect peace, whose mind is stayed on thee: because he trusteth in thee. Isaiah 26:3

While God wants to bless all believers, the capacity for managing, maximising and multiplying the blessing is dependent on your access to understanding knowledge and wisdom.

Any enterprise is built by wise planning, becomes strong through common sense, and profits wonderfully by keeping abreast of the facts. Proverbs 24:3 (Living)

3. Intellectual prosperity

This is similar to what we just referred to as mental prosperity, however this is insight, learning and understanding.

As for these four children, God gave them knowledge and skill in all learning and wisdom: and Daniel had understanding in all visions and dreams. Daniel 1:17

The great revolution coming upon our generation is in the area of intellectual prosperity. Believers must not be behind in this. Creativity, insight and wisdom are the work of the Holy Spirit and He wants to give us access into all that He can show us. The Bible says, "God will open to us the windows of heaven."

Bring ye all the tithes into the storehouse, that there may be meat in mine house, and prove me now herewith, saith the LORD of hosts, if I will not open you the windows of heaven, and pour you out a blessing, that there shall not be room enough to receive it. Malachi 3:10

Windows are designed for light to come in. We need to know what to do before we possess knowledge in our chosen field of investment. We need to know those who possess knowledge in certain areas and can be good mentors to us. We need to know how to protect the knowledge we have that makes us specialists in certain areas. However, get ready to pay the price that will make your intellectual property worth the price you demand for it.

4. Financial prosperity

For ye know the grace of our Lord Jesus Christ, that, though he was rich, yet for your sakes he became poor, that ye through his poverty might be rich. 2 Corinthians 8:9

And God is able to make all grace abound toward you; that ye, always having all sufficiency in all things, may abound to every good work: 2 Corinthians 9:8

God's mandate according to this scripture is that by reason of our commitment to Christ we have now been chosen to abound in every good work. We have now been given all of the riches of God because Christ took our place and Christ took our poverty.

HOW DO YOU WALK IN YOUR FINANCIAL MANDATE?

1. You must be covenant conscious

It is important to allow your spirit to receive your covenant rights. It is important to permit your spirit to think covenant thoughts.

My covenant will I not break, nor alter the thing that is gone out of my lips. Psalm 89:34

These thoughts include the desire of God to prosper the believer is rooted in covenant. The agreement of God to which He is committed to bless and to make good whatever He promises.

2. Recognise the law of sowing and reaping

While the earth remaineth, seedtime and harvest, and cold and heat, and summer and winter, and day and night shall not cease. Genesis 8:22

But this I say, He which soweth sparingly shall reap also sparingly; and he which soweth bountifully shall reap also bountifully. Every man according as he purposeth in his heart, so let him give; not grudgingly, or of necessity: for God loveth a cheerful giver. 2 Corinthians 9:6-7

While there is a mandate out for the believer to experience the grace and the blessing of God, yet all that God does is based on principles and laws. Once the principles are applied and the laws kept, the blessing will be released. To fail to recognise and respect the law of God is to automatically cause hindrance. Obeying God's word and walking in His will releases you into favour. This leads into another principle.

Obey the principle of the tithe in Malachi 3:10-11.

Bring ye all the tithes into the storehouse, that there may be meat in mine house, and prove me now herewith, saith the LORD of hosts, if I will not open you the windows of heaven, and pour you out a blessing, that there shall not be room enough to receive it. And I will rebuke the devourer for your sakes, and he shall not destroy the fruits of your ground; neither shall your vine cast her fruit before the time in the field, saith the LORD of hosts. Malachi 3:10-11

We have covered the subject of tithing extensively in the chapter on "The Ministry." Obedience to the principle of tithing brings you fully under the benefit of the mandate of financial prosperity. Your disobedience obviously means that you do not deserve the blessing of God.

3. Give cheerfully

Every man according as he purposeth in his heart, so let him give; not grudgingly, or of necessity: for God loveth a cheerful giver. 2 Corinthians 9:7

Again this has been covered under the chapter relating to "The Ministry." Giving is living; he who fails to give to the work of God hinders himself from receiving from the Lord.

4. Live in His presence

Whither shall I go from thy spirit? or whither shall I flee from thy presence? If I ascend up into heaven, thou art there: if I make my bed in hell, behold, thou art there. If I take the wings of the morning, and dwell in the uttermost parts of the sea; Even there shall thy hand lead me, and thy right hand shall hold me. Psalm 139:7-10

It is dangerous to depart from the presence of the Lord. Moses and Joshua could only lead the people of God into their wealthy place because they solicited and practised the act of being in the presence of God. To have a mandate for financial prosperity and live outside of the mandate of God is to turn the blessing to a desert and to negate the power and purpose of God's prosperity. The presence of God brought light for the children of Israel, where there was darkness. It brought illumination, where there was darkness. It brought direction when they were lost. It brought peace where they knew heat and trouble. The presence of God negates and expels the presence of the enemy.

The presence of God cannot dwell or cohabit perpetually with the spirit of poverty. One of the benefits of being in the presence of God is that it helps you to constantly know and follow the instruction of God. Addiction to His presence is necessary for you to fully experience His presents.

And he said, My presence shall go with thee, and I will give thee rest. Exodus 33:14

For the eyes of the LORD run to and fro throughout the whole earth, to shew himself strong in the behalf of them whose heart is perfect toward him. Herein thou hast done foolishly: therefore from henceforth thou shalt have wars. 2 Chronicles 16:9

5. Act on what you hear in His presence

The beauty of God's financial prosperity is that it is rooted in obedience to God's instruction.

His mother saith unto the servants, Whatsoever he saith unto you, do it. John 2:5

When we obey God's command we come into all that God has for us. Every time you choose to make the counsel of the Lord and the Word of the Lord your direction, things will prosper.

Blessed is the man that walketh not in the counsel of the ungodly, nor standeth in the way of sinners, nor sitteth in the seat of the scornful. But his delight is in the law of the LORD; and in his law doth he meditate day and night. And he shall be like a tree planted by the rivers of water, that bringeth forth his fruit in his season; his leaf also shall not wither; and whatsoever he doeth shall prosper. Psalm 1:1-3

However, for the man who thinks himself to be smart and chooses to walk in his own counsel, he misses the counsel of the Lord and therefore does not realise that what may appear ridiculous to the human mind, may be the stepping stone to the miraculous. Those who stay in His presence, waiting for the instruction to do what He tells them always succeed in what they carry out.

This book of the law shall not depart out of thy mouth; but thou shalt meditate therein day and night, that thou mayest observe to do according to all that is written therein: for then thou shalt make thy way prosperous, and then thou shalt have good success. Joshua 1:8

And he gave heed unto them, expecting to receive something of them. Acts 3:5

6. Prioritise kingdom business

But seek ye first the kingdom of God, and his righteousness; and all these things shall be added unto you. Matthew 6:33

This subject is also covered elsewhere, however it is important to understand that though we are under the mandate to prosper, we must understand the purpose of God's prosperity. That above every other thing, the business of His kingdom must take priority. You cannot be a tithe-eater; you cannot be a person who withholds his giving and prosper in the things of God.

7. Depend on the counsel of the Lord

Make the counsel of the Lord your chief desire and pursue it. Do not carry out any matter based on your own smartness, particularly when it comes to finance. How many people have loaned out money, or carried out financial transactions without really allowing God to lead them? The benefit to the believer of the leading of the Holy Spirit is that you cannot be led wrong.

Truly my soul waiteth upon God: from him cometh my salvation. My soul, wait thou only upon God; for my expectation is from him. Psalm 62:1,5

This in effect shows that only the counsel of the Lord can get you out of mess. Only the counsel of the Lord can get the blessing and favour and the harvest you desire.

8. Believe the promises of God to prosper you

This is paramount; having an understanding that your financial mandate comes from God and that He has made His commitment to prosper you.

9. Reject and refuse the tendency to be selfish, stingy or cheap

Three times in a year shall all thy males appear before the LORD thy God in the place which he shall choose; in the feast of unleavened bread, and in the feast of weeks, and in the feast of tabernacles: and they shall not appear before the LORD empty: Every man shall give as he is able, according to the blessing of the LORD thy God which he hath given thee. Deuteronomy 16:16-17

The chief purpose of God's prosperity is not merely to meet our need, but to provide for a vision. The primary vision of the believer should be to touch the world with God's provision. In the light of that, we cannot be selfish or stingy and continue to proper.

10. Recognise that the God we serve is an uncommon God

If our God is an unusual and uncommon God, a common lifestyle is abnormal to the supernatural. If our God is an unusual and uncommon God, His goodness cannot be following you and you remain common and broke. If His anointing is an uncommon anointing that brings ability, harvests should be increasing in your life.

His Word is an uncommon seed; if His seed is in your life then you should be producing an uncommon harvest. God made us to be an uncommon breed, particularly now that we are in Christ Jesus, so our harvest should be a bumper one.

But ye are a chosen generation, a royal priesthood, an holy nation, a peculiar people; that ye should shew forth the praises of him who hath called you out of darkness into his marvellous light: 1 Peter 2:9

First Peter 2:9 shows what stuff we are made of, that is why the scripture says, "We have been called out of darkness." Darkness in this context of our teaching on the mandate for finances stands for 'death, indebtedness, sickness, sadness and everything that reduces life and poisons your harvest.'

This ironically means that you also serve an uncommon God. You cannot be 'normal' and your harvest should not be. The mandate you carry therefore means that you should live an uncommon life. Your neighbours should be wondering what exactly makes you uncommon. They should be wondering how come you prosper with everything you lay your hands to do.

The LORD is my light and my salvation; whom shall I fear? the LORD is the strength of my life; of whom shall I be afraid? Psalm 27:1

11. Recognise that when you become committed to God you also become addicted to giving and money becomes committed to you

I beseech you, brethren, (ye know the house of Stephanas, that it is the firstfruits of Achaia, and that they have addicted themselves to the ministry of the saints,) 1 Corinthians 16:15

There is a place in God where money cannot pass by, because you live in the land of harvest. Money cannot pass by because God knows you will use it for His covenant. The commitment of money to you means in effect that if people owe you, covenant will go after them and make them pay you. If people steal from you it has to come back, and if you have been undercut and underpaid, God will restore it back.

And these are they which are sown on good ground; such as hear the word, and receive it, and bring forth fruit, some thirty fold, some sixty, and some an hundred. Mark 4:20

The perpetuation of the mandate for financial blessing requires that you act wisely with the provision of God, that even in our giving in the house of God it should be where we know to be good grounds. Not every ministry is good ground. One sure sign of good ground is where souls are saved and lives are transformed.

12. Always make God the source of your blessing and the senior partner in your life.

What makes the believer different is the understanding that his finances, business and the whole of the affairs of his life are tied into God, and that God is the senior partner.

And if children, then heirs; heirs of God, and joint-heirs with Christ; if so be that we suffer with him, that we may be also glorified together. Romans 8:17

What then? are we better than they? No, in no wise: for we have before proved both Jews and Gentiles, that they are all under sin; Romans 3:9

13. Let it be clear and established in your life that it is God's will for you to prosper

But without faith it is impossible to please him: for he that cometh to God must believe that he is, and that he is a rewarder of them that diligently seek him. Hebrews 11:6

Beloved, I wish above all things that thou mayest prosper and be in health, even as thy soul prospereth. 3 John 1:2

An understanding of the mandate that you are called to prosper should make you not to debate, doubt or deliberate the negative opinions of those who do not hold on to the belief in prosperity.

14. Make sure you honour the Lord at all times in your method, means and ministry of giving.

Honour the LORD with thy substance, and with the first fruits of all thine increase: Proverbs 3:9

Part of the recognition of the mandate of God concerning your finances is the understanding that not only should you give to the Lord, but the method, the means and the ministry of your giving must bring honour to the name of God. The actual money does not rise to heaven, but the attitude behind it and the honour you bring to God is what goes to Him. Therefore the action must be right and the method needs to be God glorifying.

15. Recognise that the wealth of God is looking for covenant people who have the anointing to handle it.

Fools, the Bible says, are destroyed by their own prosperity. Therefore the mandate of God on you requires that you handle the blessing God will send to you in a wise way. It is that ability to handle the favour and blessing of God properly that will cause the blessing to rest on you, and for you to enjoy God's provision.

If ye be willing and obedient, ye shall eat the good of the land: Isaiah 1:19

Therefore get ready to transform the coming days to that of days of heaven on earth.

That your days may be multiplied, and the days of your children, in the land which the LORD sware unto your fathers to give them, as the days of heaven upon the earth. Deuteronomy 11:21

Get ready to stop working so hard to try to make things happen, ready to stop hitch-hiking, ready to stop watering things with your foot like they did in Egypt from Bible times in the land of little supply. Be prepared to enter what God has for you, to walk in the joy of giving and the blessing of living. Understand that prosperity is by a covenant that cannot be revoked, erased or eradicated.

> *But thou shalt remember the LORD thy God: for it is he that giveth thee power to get wealth, that he may establish his covenant which he sware unto thy fathers, as it is this day. Deuteronomy 8:18*

> *My covenant will I not break, nor alter the thing that is gone out of my lips. Psalm 89:34*

The mandate on the believer to prosper and to increase in the financial blessing of God is not on the basis of skill, ability or power. Rather, the power to get wealth, make wealth, or increase rests in God who puts it on the believer because of the finished work of Christ on the cross of Calvary. Your lack of education therefore pales in the sight of the fact that God is the One who called you to prosper.

In conclusion, do not take short cuts. It is God's will for you to increase and prosper. It is important for you to find the field God has ordained and enter it for your harvest. Refuse to settle for leftovers; the mandate on you transcends such. Take your hand from the land of the present and fix it on the land of God's promise. The land of 'the present' is immediate and within your reach, it is lacking in fulfilment and cannot reach the third and fourth generations. The land of God's promise is where God is taking you from just enough to more than enough.

> *Thou hast caused men to ride over our heads; we went*

through fire and through water: but thou broughtest us out into a wealthy place. Psalm 66:12

If you live only on what you have now you will never arrive at your potential destination. There is a mandate that must produce a change in your life. Such a change will cause fruit to remain in your life.

Riches and honour are with me; yea, durable riches and righteousness. My fruit is better than gold, yea, than fine gold; and my revenue than choice silver. I lead in the way of righteousness, in the midst of the paths of judgment: That I may cause those that love me to inherit substance; and I will fill their treasures. Proverbs 8:18-21

The understanding that there is a mandate for your prosperity should make your mind be renewed and for you to exclaim with that clear Bible understanding that it is too late to be poor. It is impossible for you to be poor, and it is not in God's plan for you to be poor. Education cannot stop you, your social class is not comparable to what God wants to do, your ethnic identity has nothing to do with your mandate and your gender cannot limit you. You must possess your possession.

-5-
THE MAGNET

Why do some people seem to attract money when others repel it? Why does it seem as if money is friendlier to some people, while some others seem to be its enemy? Why does some people's money seem to have more mileage than that of others? For a comprehensive look that will give us an understanding as to why some people attract money when others repel it we will go through the book of Proverbs.

Solomon's treatise on finance in the book of Proverbs may be easily summarised into four categories: habits, attitudes, actions and belief systems. To leave no one in doubt Solomon makes it clear that God is no respecter of persons when it comes to the distribution of wealth, ability and strength; at least the essential tools are given to all men equally.

The rich and poor meet together: the LORD is the maker of them all. Proverbs 22:2

The poor and the deceitful man meet together: the LORD lighteneth both their eyes. Proverbs 29:13

These scriptures quoted give us an indication that all men are created equal. The sun does not shine on some people to a greater degree than others. All humans have equal opportunities. Where men and women ultimately find themselves is often influenced by the choices they make, habits they form, the attitudes they put on and the actions they carry out. We all have equal fingers, the same number of legs. The capacity to learn, influenced by the environment of our upbringing is largely responsible for our money habits and beliefs.

All humans have their equal share of eyes. The rich do not have more eyes or bigger brains, they just used what they had. The difference between the rich and the poor, i.e. the ability to attract or repel money is influenced by four main factors - habits, actions, attitudes and belief systems. The appropriate application of these four determines people's placement in life.

Firstly let us look at habits

A. HABITS

There are negative and positive ones. Negative habits would include fear, failure, cynicism and laziness. If you want to be a money magnet you must recognise that the negative habits can hold you down, or as a matter of fact become your lever for rising.

Negative Habits

The first negative habit towards money which we want to look at is:

1. Fear

The scriptures give us understanding that God has not given us the spirit of fear.

For God hath not given us the spirit of fear; but of power, and of love, and of a sound mind. 2 Timothy 1:7

Our money fears affect our ability to magnetise or repel money. The acronym FEAR stands for "False Evidence Appearing Real." Until you deal with your money fears you might not be able to magnetise and keep money. Money fears would include the fear of not having enough, having too much, or losing it. Money fears are often influenced by what our parents said, or what our childhood experience was. Money fears influence hoarding, and these fears could make people not give. The result is that they will not experience the miracle of God's supply.

2. Cynicism

Cynics never win at anything, they never make attempts that break out of the regular cycle. Cynics never succeed. They never take bold steps and it is impossible to be a money magnet if you are not willing to take bold steps, either in the investing of money or in the releasing of it to serve God. Those who are cynical about what God said in Bible times never receive the reward.

Had Israel been cynical of what God told Moses, they would have been buried in Egypt, no deliverance. Had Peter had been cynical when Jesus asked him to catch a fish and get his tax money out of the fish, he would have ended in jail.

Positive Habits

There are positive habits that influence and help in attracting money.

1. Diligence

Diligence is one of the cardinal teachings of the book of Proverbs.

Go to the ant, thou sluggard; consider her ways, and be wise: Proverbs 6:6

Solomon calls our attention to the fact that even little people can teach us to succeed, because if you belittle those who can teach you, you will be little. The ants teach us that smart, not size, is the key to succeeding. Sometimes people will create big organisations with large overheads and fail to realise that you can be lean and mean instead of being big and flabby. Nothing can replace diligence. Those who do not take life seriously will not make any impact, and when a man does not take life seriously he becomes indolent and nonchalant.

He becometh poor that dealeth with a slack hand: but the hand of the diligent maketh rich. Proverbs 10:4

Poverty is a product of average living. It is the result you get for dealing with a slack hand. There is no conspiracy by a government to keep people poor. The school system does not choose to keep people poor. The decision of your parents cannot keep you poor forever. The man who is careless about his enterprise will live with poverty. However, diligence will introduce you to your day of favour.

Thou shalt arise, and have mercy upon Zion: for the time to favour her, yea, the set time, is come. Psalm 102:13

Diligence is necessary for you to rule in the midst of your brethren and to stand out.

The hand of the diligent shall bear rule: but the slothful shall be under tribute. Proverbs 12:24

Society has no time to recognise or build a monument to the slothful or lazy, but rather it sends them to be sold as slaves. Lazy people do not magnetise money, rather they are known for wasted energy, resources, ideas, gifts, etc. Waste is the only mark of a lazy man.

The slothful man roasteth not that which he took in hunting: but the substance of a diligent man is precious. Proverbs 12:27

Money will only be magnetised by those who have chosen the path of diligence. Until you work, nothing around you would work, and if you want cheap success it will not take long before you discover that "easy come, easy go."

He that tilleth his land shall be satisfied with bread: but he that followeth vain persons is void of understanding. Proverbs 12:11

The law of sowing and reaping makes it clear; it is what a man sows that he can reap. It is what he puts into life that determines what he gets out of it.

Be not deceived; God is not mocked: for whatsoever a man soweth, that shall he also reap. Galatians 6:7

Some resign their future to luck and therefore try the pools, bingo, the lottery, and any short cut to wealth that they could find. However, the only guaranteed route to magnetise and keep wealth is diligence.

Diligence in the area of your chosen field. Diligence in your gift area will cause light to shine in a man's path. And all those who do not celebrate you today will come to the brightness of your shining.

The poor is hated even of his own neighbour: but the rich hath many friends. Proverbs 14:20

Results do not follow mere ideas or talk, talk is cheap. Result only follows diligent workers.

In all labour there is profit: but the talk of the lips tendeth only to penury. Proverbs 14:23

Therefore once a man finds a divine idea, a God-given idea, that idea can open a world of breakthroughs. What are we saying in effect? Find your area of specialisation and fill the area of your specialisation, and then fruits will follow.

The thoughts of the diligent tend only to plenteousness; but of every one that is hasty only to want. Proverbs 21:5

Your hand would only work out what your heart has conceived.

The desire of the slothful killeth him; for his hands refuse to labour. Proverbs 21:25

Diligence will make a man refuse to sleep when others are. He would be up answering tomorrow's questions when others are still living in the past. It will make a man prepare for the future when others have taken an early rest. Diligence makes a man push himself beyond the limit. Those who answer tomorrow's questions today will always be ahead.

Any enterprise is built by wise planning, becomes strong through common sense, and profits wonderfully by keeping abreast of the facts. Proverbs 24:3 (Living)

Magnetising money therefore requires work - working with all of your abilities; mentally, spiritually and emotionally. It is your life and therefore for you to attract and keep the wealth of God you must show that it should come to you.

He that tilleth his land shall have plenty of bread: but he that followeth after vain persons shall have poverty enough. Proverbs 28:19

Your habits will find you out, but habits will also help you to find out your future. Prosperity does not fall from the sky but it has to be worked out diligently.

And he shall be like a tree planted by the rivers of water, which bringeth forth his fruit in his season; his leaf also shall not wither; and whatsoever he doeth shall prosper. Psalm 1:3

It therefore means that mental, spiritual and physical habits necessary to achieve your goal must be explored. Studying is a habit, which must be explored in order to prove yourself in your chosen field.

Study to shew thyself approved unto God, a workman that needeth not to be ashamed, rightly dividing the word of truth. 2 Timothy 2:15

Hard work is a choice, which must be carried out.

The sleep of a labouring man is sweet, whether he eat little or much: but the abundance of the rich will not suffer him to sleep. Ecclesiastes 5:12

No man has ever died as a result of hard, intelligent work. It only renews your strength and keeps you doing what you love to do. A working man is a healthy man and nothing is more enjoyable in life than being one. After all, nothing works unless you are a worker. So the only thing that will set you up for promotion is when you are excited about your chosen field.

B. ATTITUDES

Your attitude, not aptitude, is what will determine your altitude. Doors are either open or shut permanently because of a man's attitude. Some people have been kept on for longer in an establishment because they had a good attitude, while others who seemed highly qualified have lost jobs because their attitude slammed the door in their face. Your attitude can put food on your table or take it away. It can either increase or decrease the friends in your life. Your attitude can make you stay in the game of life until you win, in spite of intense pressure. It can make you give up so soon just when you are close to the victory.

Negative Attitudes

Let us first look at negative attitudes because these sadly slam doors in our face and make us lose the opportunity to magnetise money and draw favours. Negative attitudes shut the womb of kindness and stop favour from flowing to the believer.

1. Thinking with your emotions

Riches profit not in the day of wrath: but righteousness delivereth from death. Proverbs 11:4

One of the ways we think with our emotions is when we

make decisions out of anger. The man who is always walking in anger can never increase productivity. The man who walks in anger will repel favours, he will lose all his profits, and reduce his contacts and friendships.

Be not hasty in thy spirit to be angry: for anger resteth in the bosom of fools. Ecclesiastes 7:9

2. Refusing to receive instructions

Poverty and shame shall be to him that refuseth instruction: but he that regardeth reproof shall be honoured. Proverbs 13:18

There is no money problem on earth, there is only a wisdom problem and therefore the refusal to be instructed to receive wisdom will perpetually shut one away from the blessings of God. Someone knows what you do not know, someone has answers to the questions you are asking. When you receive instruction you will kiss poverty and shame goodbye.

3. Excuses

The slothful man saith, There is a lion without, I shall be slain in the streets. Proverbs 22:13

"Excusitis" is a terrible disease, which prevents people from magnetising money. No great enterprise, barrier breaking idea, or frontier pushing action has been born out of the refusal to take risks. No one makes progress on the train of excuses. If everyone gave excuses, the Eskimos would not build igloos, planes would not be invented and they would not fly. There would be no crude oil dug from the deepest depths of the earth, no gold on our fingers, no cars on our roads or no clothes on our backs. The man who makes excuses will never change his horizon; the scenario never changes for him. He will only see the same picture.

4. Uncontrolled desires

The desire of the slothful killeth him; for his hands refuse to labour. Proverbs 21:25

The root for many people's quest for financial increase is determined not by need or the desire to bless and influence the work of God, but greed. Uncontrolled desire will make a man break laws, take actions that are unhealthy to his soul, unethical to his life and unhelpful for his future. When this is your motivation, it destroys.

5. Covetousness

He coveteth greedily all the day long: but the righteous giveth and spareth not. Proverbs 21:26

The covetous man never gives but loves to receive. The covetous man wants what is not his right to have and does not care how he gets it. He wants immediate gratification, and does not know the power of delayed gratification. He wants what belongs to the Lord and therefore steals the tithe or any other thing God requires to be given to Him. He withholds from God and man and sometimes from himself.

6. Impatience

A faithful man shall abound with blessings: but he that maketh haste to be rich shall not be innocent. Proverbs 28:20

He that hasteth to be rich hath an evil eye, and considereth not that poverty shall come upon him. Proverbs 28:22

The impatient forget that if you know God and serve Him, you can attract money without having to bend the rules, ending up in jail or with a guilty conscience. Impatience makes a man see right as wrong or wrong as right. Impatience will make a man have an evil eye until he loses everything. Other negative attitudes that will stop a man from attracting wealth are:

7. Limiting God

Yea, they turned back and tempted God, and limited the Holy One of Israel. Psalm 78:41

8. Tempting God

Yea, they turned back and tempted God, and limited the Holy One of Israel. Psalm 78:41

9. Arrogance

Some become arrogant with the little they have and since they have become high minded, they shut their ability to walk in supernatural wealth.

The rich man is wise in his own conceit; but the poor that hath understanding searcheth him out. Proverbs 28:11

Arrogance is when ego, ignorance and little money end up in the hand of a man. An arrogant man dishonours men of God and the anointing that is upon their lives. An arrogant man will also dishonour the church of God. An arrogant man is likely to be separated from the little he has.

The third thing that makes people either be money magnets or money repellent is their actions.

C. ACTIONS

Actions either draw you closer to your wealthy place or further away. Some of the actions which repel wealth and blessing are:

1. Greed

He that is greedy of gain troubleth his own house; but he that hateth gifts shall live. Proverbs 15:27

All riches that are gotten by cheating, or looking for short cuts to quick wealth will not last.

Better is a little with righteousness than great revenues without right. Proverbs 16:8

An inheritance may be gotten hastily at the beginning; but the end thereof shall not be blessed. Proverbs 20:21

Money will be repulsive and move away from the hands of the man who loves pleasure and focuses on liabilities rather than what increases wealth.

He that loveth pleasure shall be a poor man: he that loveth wine and oil shall not be rich. Proverbs 21:17

Some people are into downward investment instead of the upward. Downward investment is everything that takes away the value of your money while upward investment is whatever multiplies the value of your money.

2. Taking bribes

The king by judgment establisheth the land: but he that receiveth gifts overthroweth it. Proverbs 29:4

3. Oppressing the poor

A poor man that oppresseth the poor is like a sweeping rain, which leaveth no food. Proverbs 28:3

4. Overpricing goods for hyper profits

He that by usury and unjust gain increaseth his substance, he shall gather it for him that will pity the poor. Proverbs 28:8

Being profitable is necessary, however you cannot be a money magnet if you are looking for hyper profit. You reduce your chance of further sale and referrals.

5. Living a life of constant borrowing and being in debt

The rich ruleth over the poor, and the borrower is servant to the lender. Proverbs 22:7

We have dealt with this in another chapter in more detail. However, such actions reduce the chance of being a money magnet.

6. Taking advantage of poor people for your own wealth

He that oppresseth the poor to increase his riches, and he that giveth to the rich, shall surely come to want. Proverbs 22:16

7. Entering contracts without adequate knowledge

Be not thou one of them that strike hands, or of them that are sureties for debts. If thou hast nothing to pay, why should he take away thy bed from under thee? Proverbs 22:26-27

Haste and the inability to study the small print in contracts have made many lose millions. Some have inadvertently signed off their talents, abilities and giftings because they did not realise what they were getting into. Court actions have not been adequate to resolve and get back what some have lost in life.

Whatever you get involved in, business transactions, music, publishing, sales etc., it is important to read the small print. There are good actions that lead to wealth and the attraction of the blessings of God. There are good actions that lead to being a money magnet. It starts with building the enterprise God has put in your hands.

Any enterprise is built by wise planning, becomes strong through common sense, and profits wonderfully by keeping abreast of the facts. Proverbs 24:3 (Living)

Taking wise actions means learning to build by insight, increasing knowledge by pursuing and having enough understanding of what you are engaged in, and learning to provoke the favour of God.

Ministering to the need of the poor is also an action that attracts an increase and glorifies God. We have covered this in more detail under the chapter entitled "The Ministry." However, Solomon refers to it extensively:

There is that maketh himself rich, yet hath nothing: there is that maketh himself poor, yet hath great riches. Proverbs 13:7

He that despiseth his neighbour sinneth: but he that hath mercy on the poor, happy is he. Proverbs 14:21

He that oppresseth the poor reproacheth his Maker: but he that honoureth him hath mercy on the poor. Proverbs 14:31

He that hath pity upon the poor lendeth unto the LORD; and that which he hath given will he pay him again. Proverbs 19:17

He that giveth unto the poor shall not lack: but he that hideth his eyes shall have many a curse. Proverbs 28:27

D. BELIEF SYSTEMS

The fourth influencing factor in becoming a money magnet is your belief systems. This determines your level of blessing. If your belief is wrong, your behaviour will also be wrong. If your behaviour is wrong, what you will end up holding will also be wrong. If you want to be a money magnet, if you want to draw money, there are belief systems that must be put in place in order to have the kind of blessing and favour that will come to you.

1. You must learn to honour God and form a habit of it

Honour the LORD with thy substance, and with the first fruits of all thine increase: Proverbs 3:9

2. You have to remember that a good name is to be chosen

Let the Lord give you a name and a promotion. Titles never make you, it is a name that makes you stand out.

A good name is rather to be chosen than great riches, and loving favour rather than silver and gold. Proverbs 22:1

3. Refuse to pervert your way because you want to be wealthy

It is important to recognise that waiting for God makes you a candidate of the wealth of God.

A good name is rather to be chosen than great riches, and loving favour rather than silver and gold. Proverbs 22:1

4. Recognise the power of satisfaction

A holy dissatisfaction is necessary to make progress but a sense of contentment and satisfaction at your present level also allows God to be the one to lift you.

Better is little with the fear of the LORD than great treasure and trouble therewith. Proverbs 15:16

5. Know that it is God's blessing that will bring you to the place of wealth, to the place where you attract money

When God gives it, no sorrow comes with His blessing.

The blessing of the LORD, it maketh rich, and he addeth no sorrow with it. Proverbs 10:22

6. Recognise that God will bring great wealth to your life so you can use it to fight poverty around the world

This applies not only in your life, but wherever poverty puts men and women in chains and bondage.

The rich man's wealth is his strong city: the destruction of the poor is their poverty. Proverbs 10:15

7. Recognise the power of small beginnings

Arrogance will make a man not want to start small but always remember that you have nobody to impress. To attract money and experience the wealth of God, you must let God himself be the One to make things happen. Do not force a door open or you might have to learn to shut it back until the right time. However, you might ask, "Why start small?" Because God says so.

Though thy beginning was small, yet thy latter end should greatly increase. Job 8:7

Better is the end of a thing than the beginning thereof: and the patient in spirit is better than the proud in spirit. Ecclesiastes 7:8

Imagine a world populated with humans from the first day of creation. It would have meant that they would not know how to manage relationships, and even with only his wife, Adam messed it up. Imagine if he had to also manage a world full of humans at the time he fell.

One of the reasons to start small is because there is a dimension to the Christian that makes him know that the end has been fixed and certainly God fixed a good end. If a beautiful end has been fixed, a small beginning matters less. Small beginnings are a sign that you recognise the power of delayed gratification. Hasty gratification is a sign of childishness. Once one recognises that small beginnings do not mean that is how you will end, you entrust the future into God's hand.

So the LORD blessed the latter end of Job more than his beginning: for he had fourteen thousand sheep, and six thousand camels, and a thousand yoke of oxen, and a thousand she asses. Job 42:12

8. Recognise the importance of waiting for due season

Waiting is necessary to renew your strength. It is necessary to mature for vintage blessing. It is a sign that you have learnt the power of patience and only the patient would have the best.

Knowing this, that the trying of your faith worketh patience.But let patience have her perfect work, that ye may be perfect and entire, wanting nothing. If any of you lack wisdom, let him ask of God, that giveth to all men liberally, and upbraideth not; and it shall be given him. James 1:3-5

Those who can wait will not be put to shame.

Who shall ascend into the hill of the LORD? Or who shall stand in his holy place? Psalm 24:3

Those who can wait will have their vision worked out at the appropriate time. Only the hasty will be disappointed.

For the vision is yet for an appointed time, but at the end it shall speak, and not lie: though it tarry, wait for it; because it will surely come, it will not tarry. Habakkuk 2:3

There is a waiting period before a promotion. Do not put yourself in front until you are due in God's eyes. The man who rushes into prosperity and is not mature for it will die of obscurity which he did not prepare for. We must take a lesson from the prodigal son, who saw and pursued fame that he was not prepared for and then he experienced a famine that he did not bargain for.

9. Recognise due season

The recognition of due season helps to maximise harvest and to attract money. Jesus told the story of the talents. The talents stand for money, not the ability to dance or sing. One was given one talent, the second man and the third one five. This must be because the man with five had waited long enough and had qualified. *Matthew 25:14-28*

These wait all upon thee; that thou mayest give them their meat in due season. Psalm 104:27

The eyes of all wait upon thee; and thou givest them their meat in due season. Psalm 145:15

There is meat due for those who are patient. There is a time we have matured enough to attract a certain degree of wealth and blessing. Your due season is your time of promotion when God brings you out of obscurity into His light.

Humble yourselves therefore under the mighty hand of God, that he may exalt you in due time. 1 Peter 5:6

It is the day of the manifestation of the fruitfulness God had been preparing you for.

Nevertheless he left not himself without witness, in that he did good, and gave us rain from heaven, and fruitful seasons, filling our hearts with food and gladness. Acts 14:17

It is a time when all the seed you have sown is now beginning to bring in the harvest you need.

And let us not be weary in well doing: for in due season we shall reap, if we faint not. Galatians 6:9

What in effect am I saying? Every labour, diligence, hard work, good deed, giving and tithing has its due season. The cloud that delayed the manifestation of your sunshine does not mean it can stop the sunshine. Due seasons are intended to test your heart, if you can wait until it is time for you to receive what belongs to you.

And he humbled thee, and suffered thee to hunger, and fed thee with manna, which thou knewest not, neither did thy fathers know; that he might make thee know that man doth not live by bread only, but by every word that proceedeth out of the mouth of the LORD doth man live. Deuteronomy 8:3

Due seasons prove your worth. Due seasons show that you are ready to attract and keep the wealth of God.

Once a man is able to attract, magnetise, and keep wealth, all he has to do is to keep on working on his habits, attitudes, actions and belief systems.

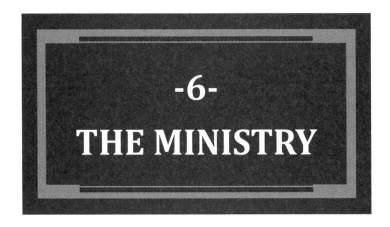

-6-
THE MINISTRY

It is important to get this aspect right because it affects every area of our finances, particularly if we understand that money without a mission can become trouble.

The foundation of a building determines its strength, the subsequent blocks laid upon it determine its longevity. In like manner, our giving to God serves as the foundation for the blessings that rest upon our lives. Our continuity in that ministry will determine the flow of the favour of God in our life. The first of all the various ways we minister to God and for God with our money is the tithe.

And Jacob rose up early in the morning, and took the stone that he had put for his pillows, and set it up for a pillar, and poured oil upon the top of it. And he called the name of that place Bethel: but the name of that city was called Luz at the first. And Jacob vowed a vow, saying, If God will be with me, and will keep me in this way that I go, and will give me bread to eat, and raiment to put on, So that I come again to my father's house in peace; then shall the LORD be my God: And this stone, which I have set for a pillar, shall be God's house: and of all that thou shalt give me I will surely give the tenth unto thee. Genesis 28:18-22

And all the tithe of the land, whether of the seed of the land, or of the fruit of the tree, is the LORD'S: it is holy unto the LORD. Leviticus 27:30

WHAT IS THE TITHE?

The tithe is 10 per cent of all of a person's increase. The word tithe means the tenth part of anything. From a biblical point of view, because it is a command, you cannot say, "Well, I think I will tithe this month and not another month." It is the principle law of bringing what has become our increase to God and on occasions when the unsaved and the unbelieving have obeyed the principle, it has worked for them because they have inadvertently triggered a spiritual law, which says that the one who brings the tithe will experience the windows of heaven open for them.

The tithe is a documentation of your faith in God; it shows that you believe in the One who commanded that the tithe should be brought. You believe that He is not a liar and He must be obeyed.

God is not a man, that he should lie; neither the son of man, that he should repent: hath he said, and shall he not do it? or hath he spoken, and shall he not make it good? Numbers 23:19

It was established by God to help man break free from the power of greed. What you are willing to walk away from determines what you walk into. The ability to walk away from the 10 per cent is a sign that one has conquered greed. There are many things that could stop you, whether it is in the managing of money or in building a strong financial base, but the key is your ability to overcome greed. If you cannot let go of the tithe, you cannot bring the blessing. And because it only produces after its own kind, greed makes you produce nothing and therefore reap nothing. Harvest responds to a law.

While the earth remaineth, seedtime and harvest, and cold and heat, and summer and winter, and day and night shall not cease. Genesis 8:22

Until your obedience is established, your financial harvest is blocked by your act of arrogance in disobeying God. Tithing is bringing back to God what belongs to Him in the first place.

And all the tithe of the land, whether of the seed of the land, or of the fruit of the tree, is the LORD'S: it is holy unto the LORD. And if a man will at all redeem ought of his tithes, he shall add thereto the fifth part thereof. And concerning the tithe of the herd, or of the flock, even of whatsoever passeth under the rod, the tenth shall be holy unto the LORD. Leviticus 27:30-32

It is a hallowed property, and by that I mean it belongs to God, entrusted to the hand of the man or woman who must bring the tithe. Your ability to bring it to God is an indication of where your heart is.

THE IMPORTANCE OF THE TITHE

Tithing is biblical, and it is a fundamental teaching of the Word of God.

And this stone, which I have set for a pillar, shall be God's house: and of all that thou shalt give me I will surely give the tenth unto thee. Genesis 28:22

The tithe is a practical action that produces a powerful result.

Tithing is a pragmatic test for which, when carried out, when the seed is sown, God promises that the degree of a person's sowing will provoke the quality of His own response.

But this I say, He which soweth sparingly shall reap also sparingly; and he which soweth bountifully shall reap also bountifully. 2 Corinthians 9:6

The believer must tithe because it is necessary for the kingdom of God to be able to make its impact on the world.

Bring ye all the tithes into the storehouse, that there may be meat in mine house, and prove me now herewith, saith the LORD of hosts, if I will not open you the windows of heaven, and pour you out a blessing, that there shall not be room enough to receive it. Malachi 3:10

Serving God with our money is an antimony. While God owns all things, yet He is unable to do many things until His people obey Him in releasing the tithe that is in their hand.

For every beast of the forest is mine, and the cattle upon a thousand hills. Psalm 50:10

Behold, the nations are as a drop of a bucket, and are counted as the small dust of the balance: behold, he taketh up the isles as a very little thing. Isaiah 40:15

Tithing is part of the believers' building block for a strong Christian life and for a future secure in obedience.

The tithe is something you owe God; it does not belong to you. When you bring it to His house, you have only returned what belongs to God. Tithing preceded the Law of Moses and therefore was established across the dispensations and across the Testaments.

And as I may so say, Levi also, who receiveth tithes, payed tithes in Abraham. For he was yet in the loins of his father, when Melchisedec met him. Hebrews 7:9-10

Tithing is necessary because it provokes the heavens to open to you. It is impossible to be blessed if you are operating under a closed heaven.

And I will rebuke the devourer for your sakes, and he shall not destroy the fruits of your ground; neither shall your vine cast her fruit before the time in the field, saith the LORD of hosts. Malachi 3:11

And all the tithe of the land, whether of the seed of the land, or of the fruit of the tree, is the LORD'S: it is holy unto the LORD. And if a man will at all redeem ought of his tithes, he shall add thereto the fifth part thereof. And concerning the tithe of the herd, or of the flock, even of whatsoever passeth under the rod, the tenth shall be holy unto the LORD. He shall not search whether it be good or bad, neither shall he change it: and if he change it at all, then both it and the change thereof shall be holy; it shall not be redeemed. Leviticus 27:30-33

Jesus would not dare minister under a closed heaven, He waited on God for 40 days and 40 nights, at the end of which the heavens opened to Him and the Father spoke.

Now when all the people were baptized, it came to pass, that Jesus also being baptized, and praying, the heaven was opened, And the Holy Ghost descended in a bodily shape like a dove upon him, and a voice came from heaven, which said, Thou art my beloved Son; in thee I am well pleased. Luke 3:21-22

When people operate under closed heavens, life is like being in an arid desert land.

It is your divine insurance against satanic encroachment.

And I will rebuke the devourer for your sakes, and he shall not destroy the fruits of your ground; neither shall your vine cast her fruit before the time in the field, saith the LORD of hosts. Malachi 3:11

The tithe establishes you in the purpose of God because more than two or three Scriptures establish it. Once two or three Scriptures establish a truth, it becomes a fundamental teaching of God's Word.

You need to tithe because Jesus endorsed it and whatever He endorsed becomes the practice of the believer.

Woe to you, scribes and Pharisees, pretenders (hypocrites)! For you give a tenth of your mint and dill and cummin and have neglected and omitted the weightier (more important) matters of the Law - right and justice and mercy and fidelity. These you ought [particularly] to have done, without neglecting the others. Matthew 23:23 (Amplified)

Jesus Himself must have been a tither. After all, He commended it in the verse just quoted.

You need to tithe because it brings deliverance from the fear to give. Once you can walk away from the one tenth, you can walk into all that God has for you.

Tithing is necessary because it is the ultimate test of devotion to God.

And he said, Lay not thine hand upon the lad, neither do thou any thing unto him: for now I know that thou fearest God, seeing thou hast not withheld thy son, thine only son from me. Genesis 22:12

The tithe is a hallowed property, touching it makes one a robber and a thief.

The depth and height of a person's worship is revealed in their ability to release what belongs to God, of which they are a steward.

Tithing is one's contribution for world evangelism. The world must be reached and the tithe is a major form of giving that makes it possible.

Bring ye all the tithes into the storehouse, that there may be meat in mine house, and prove me now herewith, saith the LORD of hosts, if I will not open you the windows of heaven, and pour you out a blessing, that there shall not be room enough to receive it. Malachi 3:10

The release of your tithe is an expression of your trust in God's ability to supply, irrespective of immediate circumstances.

In this book, I will also cover investment and managing the funds God provides. The tithe is a principle that must not be broken and because it is an investment in the God's kingdom of God you will never lose.

Refusing to tithe is an act of open rebellion and disobedience to God. The tithe is a command and not a suggestion or one of the offerings where you can chose how much you give. Partial tithe or half a tithe is no tithe. That would only make it a mere offering. The tithe is necessary because it is one of the best ways to say thank you to God for many gifts of life.

God is serious about the tithe and declares that whoever touches it is a robber.

Will a man rob God? Yet ye have robbed me. But ye say, Wherein have we robbed thee? In tithes and offerings. Ye are cursed with a curse: for ye have robbed me, even this whole nation. Bring ye all the tithes into the storehouse, that there may be meat in mine house, and prove me now herewith, saith the LORD of hosts, if I will not open you the windows of heaven, and pour you out a blessing, that there shall not be room enough to receive it. Malachi 3:8-10

It is important to walk in obedience to tithing. It opens the gateway to all that God has.

Bring ye all the tithes into the storehouse, that there may be meat in mine house, and prove me now herewith, saith the LORD of hosts, if I will not open you the windows of heaven, and pour you out a blessing, that there shall not be room enough to receive it. Malachi 3:10

The Bible talks about the windows of heaven being opened to the believer. Architects say that windows are not designed to throw things out. They are intended for bringing in the light, fresh air and to increase visibility. When you bring the tithe, imagine God opening the windows of heaven to you. The light of God's illumination comes into you.

The eyes of your understanding being enlightened; that ye may know what is the hope of his calling, and what the riches of the glory of his inheritance in the saints, Ephesians 1:18

Insight and revelation become a blessing to you and wisdom, discretion and insight will be pleasant to you.

When wisdom entereth into thine heart, and knowledge is pleasant unto thy soul; Discretion shall preserve thee, understanding shall keep thee: Proverbs 2:10-11

Freshness comes in through the window, causing or increasing ventilation. You need spiritual ventilation, the atmosphere of God's comfort and peace. Non-tithing is an attitude of arrogance and disbelieving the God who promised to respond once one tithes. Non-tithing makes one behave like an agnostic. Instead of a non-tither giving what belongs to God, he keeps it to himself, thus feeling as if he is a 'little god' himself.

Tithing helps to break the curse that may have rested upon our families. Many people are fighting their fathers' devils; the demons that have ruled in their family. Tithing is important because the seed we release is a proof of our faith in God. We need to tithe because God has a penalty for those who are thieves who steal His tithe, and instead of coming under God's penalty it is better to enjoy the prosperity God has earmarked for the obedient.

If ye be willing and obedient, ye shall eat the good of the land: Isaiah 1:19

Tithing is one of the ultimate ways to show and prove to God that we love Him and we are not just talking about it.

God gave us His Son; we must give Him what belongs to Him. One of the most powerful consequences of the tithe makes it necessary to act upon it.

It puts us in remembrance before God.

Then they that feared the LORD spake often one to another: and the LORD hearkened, and heard it, and a book of remembrance was written before him for them that feared the LORD, and that thought upon his name. Malachi 3:16

The tithe gives God the priority of being number one in our lives.

It is the opportunity to put God first by bringing Him the firstfruit, which therefore puts His protection on all the other fruit. The interesting thing about the tithe is that even people in the secular world are beginning to learn the power of giving one tenth of their profit towards charitable causes. Somehow they do not know the reason but it provokes a certain degree of blessing. In like manner, believers who are covenant children of God must recognise that the tithe is a tool for establishing your covenant relationship with God.

How deep, how high, how great your worship is, will be shown not by the talk or the song, but by your obedience. Your inner commitment must have an outer proof, and one of the ultimate expressions of such proof is the tithe you give to God. God has entrusted you with the opportunity and the sacred trust to bring the tithe yourself. Show Him that you love Him by bringing it.

The tithe is necessary because it exposes the believer to all of the favour of God, and you become a person hard to bargain with or negotiate with. Because of the favour of God on your life things would always work in your favour. The person who has not learnt to bring his tithe has not learnt to obey God in the time of sowing, therefore it would be very difficult to hear the voice of God when it is time to reap and they cannot seem to see the physical manifestation of the harvest that God has already put in place.

While we look not at the things which are seen, but at the things which are not seen: for the things which are seen are temporal; but the things which are not seen are eternal. 2 Corinthians 4:18

It is very easy for people to talk about how they love the Lord and what they can do for God. A man's cheque stub will show us how much of God he knows and how much he loves the Lord. If you know God, if you are His child you will carry His genetics. The DNA of God shows Him to be a giver and God's method of giving is liberally. God not only gives liberally, He looks for moments to make it happen. When the fullness of time came He gave us His Son. Real love waits for the moment to show itself. When the time comes, real love lavishes. The tithe is one way to lavish on God.

It is good to fast, pray and sing, but if you do not obey the first principle you miss out on your opportunity to be blessed. In effect we are saying true love must show commitment, and that commitment is expressed in the tithe. Commitment is not only when it feels right; because it is an obligation, it must be obeyed.

It is interesting that sometimes those who do not tithe will also turn to God and pray for prosperity. How can you steal from God and also ask Him to prosper you, protect, provide, promote and elevate you? It is like asking your employer who knows you are stealing from him, to give you a salary increase.

The Bible talks of a 'wealthy place,' *Thou hast caused men to ride over our heads; we went through fire and through water: but thou broughtest us out into a wealthy place. Psalm 66:12*

You cannot enter the wealthy place when you disobey the One who provided it. We quote scriptures and claim scriptures like Isaiah 54:17 that says, "No weapon formed against us will prosper," but it also says, "This is the heritage of the servants of God.." The servants of God being referred to here are those who truly serve Him with everything they have. If you want a financial testimony, you cannot eat the tithe or touch it. After all it is not yours. This is the reason God says, "Prove Me now and see if I will not open the windows of heaven."

The natural man does not find it easy to walk away from 10 per cent. So for once God asks us to prove Him.

Bring ye all the tithes into the storehouse, that there may be meat in mine house, and prove me now herewith, saith the LORD of hosts, if I will not open you the windows of heaven, and pour you out a blessing, that there shall not be room enough to receive it. Malachi 3:10

He knows that He intends to back the person who brings His tithe. What you do with a carnal blessing like money or the things you bring the tithe of, if not cash, also determines how much of God's blessing you will walk into.

THE CONSEQUENCES OF DISOBEDIENCE

God's kingdom, God's economy is unlike that of this

world where taxes are often taken at source if you work for an employer. God entrusts you with the money and leaves the ability to obey in bringing the tithe to you. However people have sometimes chosen to not obey God. They hold back the tithe.

It is important to recognise that all methods of giving are an act of personal choice, but the tithe is a command. Refusal therefore to tithe is an act of open rebellion and disobedience to God. God said it is a must once you are a child of the covenant because it establishes the covenant between you and Him.

Ye are cursed with a curse: for ye have robbed me, even this whole nation. Malachi 3:9

Following the conquest of Jericho, Israel had to confront a town called Ai. This whole nation sent a handful of armies because their enemy was so small. However unknown to them someone had touched what was set apart for God. After all Jericho was the first city, therefore it belonged to God, it was His hallowed thing. A whole nation went to war; 3 million people against 3.000 people in the town of Ai, yet the 3 million were defeated because of one man's disobedience. And that one man's disobedience cost 36 men their lives because someone had broken the agreement, the covenant that the firstfruit belongs to God. Thirty-six widows were created overnight. We do not know how many children they had. Sadly, so many orphans were now released by one man's attitude to that which belonged to God.

Achan played it cool in sin until the lot caught him. He did not even repent or change his mind; he was still reluctant to come forward. The interesting thing about the tithe is that one is given the opportunity to bring it or else he would still have to pay it, if not directly but indirectly. Achan did not repent or confess his sin, but rather pretended that nothing had happened.

Some Christians think that because God does not judge like He did in the Old Testament, He probably is different now, yet Malachi 3:6 tells us, "He does not change." So a corporate defeat because of an individual's sin came upon the whole of the nation of Israel. The people who prayed together, walked in unity, practiced unity and believed in unity would shake things. However, when one of them disobeyed in the area in which covenant is strengthened. God did not take it lightly.

Achan's sin brought a corporate curse. It must be what is reflected in Malachi 3:9, "Even this whole nation." So if you know any non-tithers you need to help them obey the Lord because God is not caught short by their non-tithing, they are the ones who lose out, miss out and are walking under the canopy of a broken covenant.

The New Testament equivalent of Achan must be Annanias and Sapphira who walked in half-truth and claimed that they had brought everything, therefore deceiving themselves and trying to deceive the people of God. What an individual does with their tithe matters to the rest of the people in the congregation. It is my conviction that the level of the people who tithe in a local church is also a determining factor of the level of blessing that flows in that church. If 30 per cent of the local church tithes, they come into30 fold blessing. If 50 per cent tithe, they come into 50 fold blessing. If you notice Deuteronomy 28 combines the blessing and the curse and it was pronounced upon a whole nation. If they triggered the blessing through obedience it came on the whole nation, so did the curse if they walked in disobedience. So that whole passage was spoken for a whole body not just an individual. In like manner when we bring the tithe in a body of a local church, one non-tither, which God calls a robber in our midst, makes us all robbers. The whole nation is what the scripture says in Malachi 3:10. After all a little leaven leaveneth the whole lump.

A little leaven leaveneth the whole lump. Galatians 5:9

Non-tithing is robbing God and when you rob God you allow the enemy to influence your own finances, because protection is removed from what is left, therefore causing the devourer to come in and steal.

They say unto him, Caesar's. Then saith he unto them, Render therefore unto Caesar the things which are Caesar's; and unto God the things that are God's. Matthew 22:21

A refusal to tithe is an act of showing your ignorance of God's instruction, walking in disobedience and suffering from God's concrete justice. One may not be able to speculate as to what is in the mind of a non-tither, however it is possible that some probably think that God will not do what He said. Others may think that the act of tithing might not work for them and some are afraid to give up what they see for what they cannot see.

Non-tithing is as a result of ignorance of God's Word and when you do not know the Word of God, you miss your covenant rights and blessings. Our responsibility and calling is to be the sponsors of the gospel. One of the ways this is done is by bringing our tithe to His house, which is the store. People do not tithe sometimes because they walk in fear.

The command to bring the tithe must not be ignored until we are sure it will work. It is our responsibility to just obey the Lord. Fear is often rooted in greed and selfishness, and selfishness makes us want to keep it all for ourselves. Selfishness ends up closing the windows of heaven, limiting the flow of blessing and making us miss greater things that God wants to do.

Sometimes people do not give also because they have listened to current sayings, cultural statements and religious lies.

There are cultural statements in town like, "All that preachers want is your money." Your obedience to tithing is not your obedience to a man, but to God. Once you have brought your tithe, you leave the man of God in the hands of God Himself to deal with. When we do not tithe we commit theft and the scripture is very clear that thieves cannot make heaven.

> But lay up for yourselves treasures in heaven, where neither moth nor rust doth corrupt, and where thieves do not break through nor steal: Matthew 6:20

It is interesting that people who think that their worship is complete without the tithe, fail to realise that fancy speeches and lofty promises and a lot of "someday I'll do this and someday I'll do that" are promises that are not good enough until commitment is shown. That commitment is by bringing the tithe as the scriptures command.

> And all the tithe of the land, whether of the seed of the

land, or of the fruit of the tree, is the LORD'S: it is holy unto the LORD.   Leviticus 27:30

If you fail to bring it, God says you must redeem it when the time comes with a higher per cent.

And if a man will at all redeem ought of his tithes, he shall add thereto the fifth part thereof. Leviticus 27:31

It is better to obey God by bringing the tithe, than to use it. Because if you use it, you may not be despised as a thief, but you would have to restore what you stole.

But if he be found, he shall restore sevenfold; he shall give all the substance of his house. Proverbs 6:31

If anything should make a man tithe, the greatest consequence is when the scripture says, "one is cursed with a curse."

Ye are cursed with a curse: for ye have robbed me, even this whole nation. Malachi 3:9

You must remember that the position of the One who curses   determines if it alights and how powerful it is. A man cannot be cursed by God and think he will survive the curse. So the tithe is not for postponement, defilement or consumption, it is for bringing.

THE BLESSING OF THE TITHE

The tithe is a covenant action instigated by God between Him and man with the intention to prosper, bless and increase man in return for his obedience. God reacts unfavourably to the man who does not tithe, but for those who tithe He promises to go all lengths, opening windows of heaven and releasing uncommon blessing into their lives.

Obedience to the tithe determines the degree of God's blessing and favour which comes upon our lives.

But this I say, He which soweth sparingly shall reap also sparingly; and he which soweth bountifully shall reap also bountifully. 2 Corinthians 9:6

When a man tithes the name of God is manifested and made great, in such a person's life.

For from the rising of the sun even unto the going down of the same my name shall be great among the Gentiles; and in every place incense shall be offered unto my name, and a pure offering: for my name shall be great among the heathen, saith the LORD of hosts. Malachi 1: 11

This blessing rests upon the tither irrespective of his geographical location; after all it is the obedience that triggers the blessing, it is that obedience that releases the favour.

Tithing is a form of renewal of the contract of peace in life.

My covenant was with him of life and peace; and I gave them to him for the fear wherewith he feared me, and was afraid before my name. Malachi 2: 5

The bringing of the tithe releases intimacy with God and serves as a defence, a line drawn around the believer to protect him from satanic encroachment.

When a believer walks in obedience and brings the tithe he sets in motion the atmosphere for God to raise a swift attack against whatever opposes His obedient child.

Victory is guaranteed for the believer against whom

injustice has risen when he has walked in the obedience of tithing.

> *And I will come near to you to judgment; and I will be a swift witness against the sorcerers, and against the adulterers, and against false swearers, and against those that oppress the hireling in his wages, the widow, and the fatherless, and that turn aside the stranger from his right, and fear not me, saith the LORD of hosts. Malachi 3:5*

Moses coveted the presence of God; this is probably the greatest thing you should covet, more than His power, because when you have His presence you have his power. That presence of God is a blessing that follows obedient tithers.

> *Even from the days of your fathers ye are gone away from mine ordinances, and have not kept them. Return unto me, and I will return unto you, saith the LORD of hosts. But ye said, Wherein shall we return? Malachi 3:7*

Windows are made for illumination. In like manner when we tithe there will be in flow of divine ideas, creativity, freshness of thought and revelation into the life of the tither.

> *Bring ye all the tithes into the storehouse, that there may be meat in mine house, and prove me now herewith, saith the LORD of hosts, if I will not open you the windows of heaven, and pour you out a blessing, that there shall not be room enough to receive it. Malachi 3:10*

The blessing that overflows is the portion of the man who obeys God in his tithe. Tithing guarantees a termination to everything which wastes and devours what God has provided.

And I will rebuke the devourer for your sakes, Malachi 3:11

And I will restore to you the years that the locust hath eaten, the cankerworm, and the caterpiller, and the palmerworm, my great army which I sent among you. Joel 2:25

The tithe provokes a reaping of a full harvest because all devourers are rebuked for you, therefore there shall be no wastage.

The tither will find that everything he starts reaches maturity, completion and fruition.

And I will rebuke the devourer for your sakes, and he shall not destroy the fruits of your ground; neither shall your vine cast her fruit before the time in the field, saith the LORD of hosts. Malachi 3:11

And I will rebuke the devouring locus for you...Malachi 3:11 (Ber)

For your sake I will forbid the locus to destroy your crops; And the vine in the field will not be barren, says the Lord of hosts. Malachi 3:11 (Bas)

And he shall be like a tree planted by the rivers of water, that bringeth forth his fruit in his season; his leaf also shall not wither; and whatsoever he doeth shall prosper. Psalm 1:3

The whole of the book of Malachi centres around the worship of the believer in the bringing of the covenant of the tithe. Malachi 3:16 makes us understand that when you bring your tithe a book of remembrance is opened before God, so that nothing you do will be forgotten,

Then they that feared the LORD spake often one to another: and the LORD hearkened, and heard it, and a book of remembrance was written before him for them that feared the LORD, and that thought upon his name. Malachi 3:16

You must remember here that it was that book of remembrance in the natural that brought Mordecai's good deed to bear when it was time to promote him.

The tithe provokes and guarantees a blessing upon generations to come.

And the LORD appeared unto him the same night, and said, I am the God of Abraham thy father: fear not, for I am with thee, and will bless thee, and multiply thy seed for my servant Abraham's sake. Genesis 26:24

One of the blessings of the tithe is the increase you bring on your life and your walk with God, as you obey God with the tithe.

Then Isaac sowed in that land, and received in the same year an hundredfold: and the LORD blessed him. And the man waxed great, and went forward, and grew until he became very great: for he had possession of flocks, and possession of herds, and great store of servants: and the Philistines envied him. Genesis 26:12-14

When you bring the tithe the curse of generational poverty and lack is broken in your family by reason of your obedience.

Christ hath redeemed us from the curse of the law, being made a curse for us: for it is written, Cursed is every one that hangeth on a tree: Galatians 3:13

Therefore the curse cannot alight on your home, it only alights on the one who does not tithe.

Ye are cursed with a curse: for ye have robbed me, even this whole nation. Malachi 3:9

When the believer brings the tithe, his actions shows gratitude, therefore God will change his altitude. God will change his positioning.

And it shall come to pass, if thou shalt hearken diligently unto the voice of the LORD thy God, to observe and to do all his commandments which I command thee this day, that the LORD thy God will set thee on high above all nations of the earth: Deuteronomy 28:1

And the LORD shall make thee the head, and not the tail; and thou shalt be above only, and thou shalt not be beneath; Deuteronomy 28:13a

The tithe is God's trigger for releasing a blanket of protection on all that belongs to you.

You have a right to claim no more miscarriage, no more destruction, no more devouring, when you have walked in obedience. The tithe places you in the legal position to receive the blessing of God.

And I will rebuke the devourer for your sakes, and he shall not destroy the fruits of your ground; neither shall your vine cast her fruit before the time in the field, saith the LORD of hosts. Malachi 3:11

The level of the corporate obedience in a local church, determines the corporate blessing that would rest upon the church and the individuals in it.

> *Ye are cursed with a curse: for ye have robbed me, even this whole nation. And I will rebuke the devourer for your sakes, and he shall not destroy the fruits of your ground; neither shall your vine cast her fruit before the time in the field, saith the LORD of hosts. Malachi 3:9,11*

This is because God thinks and speaks of His church as a nation and as one family. The blessings in the scriptures have a corporate application.   Oftentimes God will speak to a whole nation, although we claim it for our individual benefit. While this is right, yet we must know that corporate obedience only provokes a greater blessing upon a people. Whenever Israel obeyed corporately, the degree of favour upon her was major. It therefore means in effect that just as Achan caused a corporate defeat, today's Achans who withhold their tithes can bring corporate hindrance. Malachi 3 is about blessing the whole nation, the whole congregation, and the whole people. When we raise our level of obedience, God says we get ourselves ready to come into a blessing of "no room enough"

> *Bring ye all the tithes into the storehouse, that there may be meat in mine house, and prove me now herewith, saith the LORD of hosts, if I will not open you the windows of heaven, and pour you out a blessing, that there shall not be room enough to receive it. Malachi 3:10b*

It is this lack of obedience that leaves all of us with still more room to receive, because we have not entered the level of obedience God requires. The church of the latter days will only be able to have the provision for her vision when the members of the body fully understand why God blesses them and that it is in order to obey Him and promote His kingdom.

The Bible talks of power where there is unity.

Behold, how good and how pleasant it is for brethren to dwell together in unity! It is like the precious ointment upon the head, that ran down upon the beard, even Aaron's beard: that went down to the skirts of his garments; As the dew of Hermon, and as the dew that descended upon the mountains of Zion: for there the LORD commanded the blessing, even life for evermore. Psalm 133:1-3

There is a high dimension of outpouring of blessing. People move to another level in such congregations where there is corporate unity. This does not negate the power of the individual obedience that will certainly bring a blessing, yet if we have one mind and one commitment, if we walk in unity and obedience, we will bring ourselves as a group of people into another level of blessing beyond we have ever known.

There will be corporate healing, corporate deliverance and God will release favour. Many times people will ask why the church in the Acts of Apostles was so successful in its outreach, prayers etc., yet all through the Acts of Apostles, one of the things we see was that the church enjoyed corporate obedience. The result of course was that their prayer burst the prisons. Obedience, brought thousands to salvation in one day and caused incredible miracles to happen. They saw dead men walking again because of their corporate obedience.

And they, continuing daily with one accord in the temple, and breaking bread from house to house, did eat their meat with gladness and singleness of heart, Praising God, and having favour with all the people. And the Lord added to the church daily such as should be saved. Acts 2:46-47

And with great power gave the apostles witness of the resurrection of the Lord Jesus: and great grace was upon them all. Neither was there any among them that lacked: for as many as were possessors of lands or houses sold them, and brought the prices of the things that were sold, And laid them down at the apostles' feet: and distribution was made unto every man according as he had need. Acts 4:33-35

It would be lovely for a group of people to walk in the kind of blessing which God said He wants to bring upon His people in Deuteronomy 28:1-13.

This ultimate goal of 100 per cent corporate blessing is a fruit of a 100 per cent corporate obedience.

Bringing your tithe perpetuates the blessing of God upon your life.

For the children of Israel, their shoes did not wear out. This is a perpetuation of blessing. Not only was it perpetual, it was also peculiar. The bringing of the tithe will maintain God's provision. Obedience in tithing is so powerful that it triggers a continuous flow of the grace and favour of God. We see an example of the blessing and the favour of the tithe in Abraham as he obeyed God and brought the tithe. God also caused him to come into the wealthy place.

And blessed be the most high God, which hath delivered thine enemies into thy hand. And he gave him tithes of all. Genesis 14:20

Abraham of course practiced tithing and must have perpetuated it for his son to see. The blessing included an overflow of great favour on the life of his son Isaac.

Then Isaac sowed in that land, and received in the same year an hundredfold: and the LORD blessed him. And the man waxed great, and went forward, and grew until he became very great: For he had possession of flocks, and possession of herds, and great store of servants: and the Philistines envied him. Genesis 26:12-14

The tithe is God's method for guaranteeing your blessing and ensuring that wicked arrows of the enemy go back to the sender.

Obeying God in the tithe therefore bringing something into His storehouse enlists you for God's financial miracles. Boundaries are removed and global favour is shown, with doors opening everywhere when you obey God in the tithe.

And all nations shall call you blessed: for ye shall be a delightsome land, saith the LORD of hosts. Malachi 3:12

The bringing of the tithe also influences the degree of happiness you experience in your life.

And all nations shall call you blessed: for ye shall be a delightsome land, saith the LORD of hosts. Malachi 3:12

The man who walks in obedience pleasures God and therefore becomes God's treasure.

The irony is that when you become His treasure you are untouchable to the enemy.

And they shall be mine, saith the LORD of hosts, in that day when I make up my jewels; and I will spare them, as a man spareth his own son that serveth him. Malachi 3:17

God also promises to put a difference between those who serve Him and those who do not know Him. Particularly when a man serves Him with the tithe.

Then shall ye return, and discern between the righteous and the wicked, between him that serveth God and him that serveth him not. Malachi 3:18

A man who walks in obedience to the tithe has released the healing virtues of Jesus.

But unto you that fear my name shall the Sun of righteousness arise with healing in his wings; and ye shall go forth, and grow up as calves of the stall. Malachi 4:2

The believer who tithes can call upon God to reverse the setbacks experienced and turn it to victory.

And ye shall tread down the wicked; for they shall be ashes under the soles of your feet in the day that I shall do this, saith the LORD of hosts. Malachi 4:3

Tithing increases your floodgate of blessing, so you can be a greater blessing to others.

And Abram went up out of Egypt, he, and his wife, and all that he had, and Lot with him, into the south. And Abram was very rich in cattle, in silver, and in gold. Genesis 13:1-2

Once the tithe goes out of your hand, an automatic covering is released on everything you have.

The tithe is the chain in the hand of the believer for binding the enemy and thief from stealing.

The thief cometh not, but for to steal, and to kill, and to destroy: I am come that they might have life, and that they might have it more abundantly. John 10:10

The tithe places you in the legal position to receive blessings from God.

And I will rebuke the devourer for your sakes, and he shall not destroy the fruits of your ground; neither shall your vine cast her fruit before the time in the field, saith the LORD of hosts. Malachi 3:11

The tithe is your key for tapping into increase and multiplication. God's method supersedes natural laws of increase.

Bring ye all the tithes into the storehouse, that there may be meat in mine house, and prove me now herewith, saith the LORD of hosts, if I will not open you the windows of heaven, and pour you out a blessing, that there shall not be room enough to receive it. Malachi 3:10

Tithers have access to the school of the Holy Spirit who gives creativity and a better way to do things once obedience is in place.

Bring ye all the tithes into the storehouse, that there may be meat in mine house, and prove me now herewith, saith the LORD of hosts, if I will not open you the windows of heaven, and pour you out a blessing, that there shall not be room enough to receive it. Malachi 3:10

The believer who tithes can expect the best that God has. No man will give stone to his obedient children but bread as they request.

If ye be willing and obedient, ye shall eat the good of the land: Isaiah 1:19

The act of tithing makes you experience dominion over the curse of lack.

The LORD shall open unto thee his good treasure, the heaven to give the rain unto thy land in his season, and to bless all the work of thine hand: and thou shalt lend unto many nations, and thou shalt not borrow. Deuteronomy 28:12

Tithing helps you to take authority in the financial realm and to establish your prosperity in the earthly realm.

If they obey and serve him, they shall spend their days in prosperity, and their years in pleasures. Job 36:11

How To Tithe

Honour the tithe. Abraham did, Jesus did, you must and you must do it consistently. Recognise every tithe in your hand as a seed of obedience and your actions as an act of faith that will create the momentum for your destiny.

Tithe consistently

If you must experience a consistent harvest, you must establish a rhythm in your giving also. However there are people that will complain that they have been tithing and not receiving any blessing. When you check you will observe that the tendency was that they have been erratic in their giving and unpredictable in their sowing. Imagine if that was a farm. Erratic sowing would also mean erratic reaping.

Learn to walk with what the scriptures would call honouring the Lord with your substance, because that is what causes you to come into the blessing.

Honour the LORD with thy substance, and with the firstfruits of all thine increase: So shall thy barns be filled with plenty, and thy presses shall burst out with new wine. Proverbs 3:9-10

The word honour is reserved for those who we want to "respect, venerate, and defer to"; therefore the Bible says that in bringing the tithe, it must be an act of honour. Please remember that the substance stays on earth, it is the honour that rises to God and therefore God watches to see that we honour Him as we do it.

The beauty of tithing is that once the tithe goes from your hand, the rest is sanctified. Sanctified money goes further than the unsanctified.

11 QUESTIONS ABOUT THE TITHE

1. Is the tithe not only for those under the law?

Bringing the tithe to God was practiced prior to the law of Moses. We observe in the Old Testament that prior to the giving of the Law of Moses, Abraham gave the tithe to Melchizedec, the high priest of the Most High. Abraham offered his firstborn "by promise" to God. We also observe that Jacob promised to bring one tenth of all the proceeds from his journey to God. And in the New Testament Jesus encouraged the bringing of the tithe.

Woe to you, scribes and Pharisees, pretenders (hypocrites)! For you give a tenth of your mint and dill and cummin, and have neglected and omitted the weightier (more important) matters of the

Law--right and justice and mercy and fidelity. These you ought [particularly] to have done, without neglecting the others. Matthew 23:23 (Amplified Bible)

"How terrible it will be for you teachers of religious law and you Pharisees. Hypocrites! For you are careful to tithe even the tiniest part of your income, but you ignore the

important things of the law--justice, mercy, and faith. You should tithe, yes, but you should not leave undone the more important things. Matthew 23:23 (NLT)

2. Should I tithe gross or net?

The debate about tithing gross or net comes up regularly, however we must look at the need to tithe off the gross because of the fact that your real income is the gross and not the net. Secondly many times the difference is not really glaring, your gross and your net income is oftentimes a little difference. For example if you earned £130 and your take home was £100, the tithe difference on both is £3 and you do not want to short change yourself. My conclusion therefore is that it is gross not to tithe gross.

3. Could I tithe when I can afford it?

God has never asked for what you do not have. However, the tithe is about covenant; it is also about the first of all you have. You cannot put God first and be the last. You cannot put God first and be unblessed. Obedience to God is not only in the bringing of the tithe, but also in taking it before any other expense.

And Samuel said, Hath the LORD as great delight in burnt offerings and sacrifices, as in obeying the voice of the LORD? Behold, to obey is better than sacrifice, and to hearken than the fat of rams. 1 Samuel 15:22

4. Why does the church need to record my giving?

The practice of recording people's giving is not universal and therefore reasons given by churches would differ from one church to the other. However, record keeping is biblical and started with God. We observe that God would give details of what was needed to create things, or to make things happen. Solomon kept records of what it cost to build a temple. Jesus took note on the record of what the widow gave.

Record keeping is good because it is a mark of accountability and integrity. Record keeping is your best answer to false accusation.

5. Can I distribute my tithe to my favourite ministries?

In Malachi, the statement which follows the instruction to bring the tithe also shows us where it may be brought. It says "that there may be meat in mine house". That immediately indicates that it is where the worshipper meets God, the home church of the believer. So the tithe in effect means where you worship God and where you receive ministry. After all, the tithe was meant to be an instrument for the worship of God. Your favourite ministry may be a good ground where other seed may be sown; vows, pledges, offerings, prophetic offerings may be given to other ministries, but the tithe must be brought to the house where meat has to be provided for you.

That in effect is your primary place of worship. The church you consider as your covering.

6. Can I use my tithe to feed the poor?

The tithe is a sacred property belonging to God. You cannot borrow to satisfy a particular use. Using the tithe to feed the poor is to fall short of understanding that it does not belong to you in the first place and therefore you cannot determine its usage. The Bible does say to help the poor and to give alms to them, but alms are different from the tithe.

7. Why can't I give what I can afford, after all God understands?

How true, God does understand, and that is why He gave the opportunity to the believer to give what he can afford as offering. But the tithe is specific, the very word suggest one tenth of your income. That number is what God has chosen as a symbol of covenant. It is a principle, a law that cannot be broken. Obedience to it releases a blessing, and disobedience releases a curse.

8. Can I use it to buy Christian books and tapes?

We have already established the fact that the tithe is a hallowed thing; God's property. It is not to be used by the individual for the buying of books or tapes; it would still be an act of touching God's property when you do that.

9. Why can't I use it to redeem my vow?

The vow is an act of promise, pledge or commitment before God, where we choose what we want to do for God. The tithe, offering and vows are like ball games. Different rules apply to each one. If you kick the ball in basketball it is a foul. If you grab the ball in soccer with your hand, it is a foul. To use the vow to redeem your tithe, or to use the tithe to redeem your vow is also most inappropriate, because different principles undergird them.

10. Should not the focus on tithing be on weightier matters such as justice, mercy and faith?

When Jesus commented on the tithe in Matthew 23:23, His emphasis certainly was on justice, mercy and faith, but He also said that it must be carried out without neglecting the tithe.

*Woe to you, scribes and Pharisees, pretenders (hypocrites)!
For you give a tenth of your mint and dill and cummin, and
have neglected and omitted the weightier (more
important) matters of the Law--right and justice and
mercy and fidelity. These you ought [particularly] to have
done, without neglecting the others. Matthew 23:23
(Amplified)*

So balance must be brought, tithing must be done and the
works of justice, mercy and faith must not suffer.

11. Should I tithe as a business person?

This question is very broad, but the simplest answer
would be to first of all bring order to your business, so that
the capital and your outgoings are clearly differentiated
from your profit. The tithe should come from the profit, not
out of your capital, borrowings or your outgoings. After all
it is from the increase that God says you should honour Him.
Those who lean on their own understanding hurt their
tithing.

THE STEWARDSHIP OF GIVING

Giving does not sit well with the nature of man; generally
humans would prefer to keep everything they get. In the
words of John Avanzini, people would prefer to "Get all they
can, can all they get and sit on the can."

*There is that scattereth, and yet increaseth; and there is
that withholdeth more than is meet, but it tendeth to
poverty. The liberal soul shall be made fat: and he that
watereth shall be watered also himself. Proverbs 11:24-25*

One needs to understand that God blesses us so we can
provide for the needs of our family, enjoy our life on earth,
but also to be a blessing to others. He wants us to be a

conduit, a pipeline through which He can reach people who are thirsty, broken and in need of being wet with the blessing of God.

For I will pour water upon him that is thirsty, and floods upon the dry ground: I will pour my spirit upon thy seed, and my blessing upon thine offspring: Isaiah 44:3

When the poor and needy seek water, and there is none, and their tongue faileth for thirst, I the LORD will hear them, I the God of Israel will not forsake them. I will open rivers in high places, and fountains in the midst of the valleys: I will make the wilderness a pool of water, and the dry land springs of water. Isaiah 41:17-18

We are not meant to be mere reservoirs that hold on to the blessing, but those who will pass it for others too to enjoy. When God called Abraham, He said He would bless him to be a blessing to his generation.

The word blessing in Genesis 12:2 does not stand for increment alone, it also means empowerment.

And I will make of thee a great nation, and I will bless thee, and make thy name great; and thou shalt be a blessing. Genesis 12:2

In effect it means being empowered to empower others. God said, I will bless you, and you will be a blessing to others. One of the true tests of maturity in the Christian faith is your ability to walk away from what you have, as you use it in blessing other people. It is the evidence that you have received the giving nature of God, because God is a giver. Our ability to release what is in our hand, reveals the nature of our Father, who Himself is a giver.

He that spared not his own Son, but delivered him up for us all, how shall he not with him also freely give us all things? Romans 8:32

WHY GIVE?

The whole of Christianity itself was born in the womb of reaching out and giving and therefore the act of giving expresses that great dimension of the Christian faith.

For God so loved the world, that he gave his only begotten Son, that whosoever believeth in him should not perish, but have everlasting life. John 3:16

The process of giving and receiving is what makes the cycle of life be perpetuated and be enjoyable. Those who keep it to themselves do not increase. As much as seedless grapes are enjoyable to eat and nutritious to the body, their inability to reproduce themselves means that they end with one generation and with one usage.

When the body is given food, not only does the body give out energy for life, it also releases the wastage. So in effect the body received and the body gave. When the body fails to give out wastage, what was enjoyed in eating becomes a painful experience in the inability to release the waste. We need to understand why we must give, because once the understanding is appreciated, once we come into a revelation of the power of giving, the action become imperative.

We need to give because in all of God's dealings with us, His chief desire, even in our giving, is for our benefit, our own good, and whatever He provides will promote joy in our lives. God wants us to give because His instruction concerning giving is meant to bring blessings to us.

Give, and it shall be given unto you; good measure, pressed down, shaken together, and running over, shall men give into your bosom. For with the same measure that ye mete withal it shall be measured to you again. Luke 6:38

Giving increases our credit account with God.

Not because I desire a gift: but I desire fruit that may abound to your account. Philippians 4:17 (Amplified)

God motivates us to give because of the profit which He knows will come into our lives as we walk in obedience.

If they obey and serve him, they shall spend their days in prosperity, and their years in pleasures. Job 36:11

If ye be willing and obedient, ye shall eat the good of the land: Isaiah 1:19

God gave us His Son because He loved us. We give to people because we love them. We must continue to give because it is an expression of love.

Giving is a mark of maturity and the quality of your giving is a sign of how more like God you are becoming.

If ye then, being evil, know how to give good gifts unto your children, how much more shall your Father which is in heaven give good things to them that ask him? Matthew 7:11

Giving is a mark of our detachment from earthly possessions and our attachment to the person of God.

Giving serves as a bridge that connects us to other people's blessing.

And I will make of thee a great nation, and I will bless thee, and make thy name great; and thou shalt be a blessing: Genesis 12:2

As we respond in giving our covenant, God establishes the fact that not only will He bless us but also He empowers us to be a blessing.

> *Now the LORD had said unto Abram, Get thee out of thy country, and from thy kindred, and from thy father's house, unto a land that I will shew thee: And I will make of thee a great nation, and I will bless thee, and make thy name great; and thou shalt be a blessing: And I will bless them that bless thee, and curse him that curseth thee: and in thee shall all families of the earth be blessed. Genesis 12:1-3*

Giving is necessary because it helps the believer to establish the purpose of God on earth, and that purpose can only be carried out through the preaching of the Word, and the Word can only go forth if a preacher has been sent.

> *How then shall they call on him in whom they have not believed? and how shall they believe in him of whom they have not heard? and how shall they hear without a preacher? And how shall they preach, except they be sent? as it is written, How beautiful are the feet of them that preach the gospel of peace, and bring glad tidings of good things! But they have not all obeyed the gospel. For Esaias saith, Lord, who hath believed our report? So then faith cometh by hearing, and hearing by the word of God. Romans 10:14-17*

Believers need to give because it helps to reach the lost. Those who are committed to the spreading of the gospel must recognise that this great cause would only be possible from the giving of the believers. Giving is necessary because it is what establishes financial blessing in the life of a

Christian. The force of financial blessing is released as we give our money.

But this I say, He which soweth sparingly shall reap also sparingly; and he which soweth bountifully shall reap also bountifully. 2 Corinthians 9:6

Giving is the planting of a financial seed in order to experience a financial harvest.

It is impossible to reap a harvest of the seed you have not sown. The farmer who complains and limits the seed he sows or plants has also limited the harvest he will have. In the same vein the farmer who plants a bountiful seed has a right to expect a bountiful harvest.

Be not deceived; God is not mocked: for whatsoever a man soweth, that shall he also reap. Galatians 6:7

Your level of harvest cannot be divorced from your level of giving.

Give, and it shall be given unto you; good measure, pressed down, and shaken together, and running over, shall men give into your bosom. For with the same measure that ye mete withal it shall be measured to you again. Luke 6:38

God has put in place an inviolable law that seed must produce after its own kind.

And God said, Let the earth bring forth grass, the herb yielding seed, and the fruit tree yielding fruit after his kind, whose seed is in itself, upon the earth: and it was so. And the earth brought forth grass, and herb yielding seed after his kind, and the tree yielding fruit, whose seed was in itself, after his kind: and God saw that it was good. Genesis 1:11-12

God has put in place an inviolable law that seedtime and harvest time would not cease.

While the earth remaineth, seedtime and harvest, and cold and heat, and summer and winter, and day and night shall not cease. Genesis 8:22

Our giving is one of the highest forms of sacrificial worship. So when we give we are participating in the process of creating a financial future.

While the earth remaineth, seedtime and harvest, and cold and heat, and summer and winter, and day and night shall not cease. Genesis 8:22

Giving is a principle of prosperity in contradiction to secular opinions, but which provokes the blessing of the Lord.

There is that scattereth, and yet increaseth; and there is that withholdeth more than is meet, but it tendeth to poverty. The liberal soul shall be made fat: and he that watereth shall be watered also himself. Proverbs 11:24-25

In effect it means, that while many think that it is by hoarding that you increase, the Bible says releasing is what brings increasing.

Giving honours God as the Lord of all.

Wherefore David blessed the LORD before all the congregation: and David said, Blessed be thou, LORD God of Israel our father, for ever and ever. Thine, O LORD, is the greatness, and the power, and the glory, and the victory, and the majesty: for all that is in the heaven and in the earth is thine; thine is the kingdom, O LORD, and thou art exalted as head above all. Both riches and honour come of thee, and thou reignest over all; and in thine hand is power and might; and in thine hand it is to make great, and to give strength unto all. Now therefore, our God, we thank thee, and praise thy glorious name. But who am I, and what is my people, that we should be able to offer so willingly after this sort? for all things come of thee, and of thine own have we given thee. O LORD our God, all this store that we have prepared to build thee an house for thine holy name cometh of thine hand, and is all thine own. 1 Chronicles 29:10-14, 16

Giving is an instrument for the establishment of the covenant between you and God.

The Lord Jesus said, "It is more blessed to give than to receive." Possibly because it is a sign of maturity to be able to give away. One of the most powerful tools for the warfare of life is giving. It opens the windows of heaven, it rebukes every financial devourer, and it stops them dead in their tracks. Giving becomes your powerful seed for a future of a great harvest. It is not an act that is carried out flippantly, but must be thought through and prayerfully approached.

It is the most powerful principle of God designed to be a blessing to both the giver and the recipient. The natural mind may not understand it - it cannot see how letting go will lead to receiving abundance. However, God's Word stands that it is the one who scatters that increases. The unscriptural mind thinks hoarding is the answer and that giving away what you have decreases your net worth, but yet God says it is in that act of giving that we increase.

WHAT SHOULD WE GIVE?

1. Freewill offering

This is called the freewill offering because it involves the action of your will. In other words you are involved in determining the amount to be given.

Therefore if thou bring thy gift to the altar, and there rememberest that thy brother hath ought against thee; Matthew 5:23

The wilderness church, which is Israel while travelling to Canaan land, was taught never to appear before the Lord empty handed.

Three times in a year shall all thy males appear before the LORD thy God in the place which he shall choose; in the feast of unleavened bread, and in the feast of weeks, and in the feast of tabernacles: and they shall not appear before the LORD empty: Every man shall give as he is able, according to the blessing of the LORD thy God which he hath given thee. Deuteronomy 16:16-17

This is a principle of kingdoms. We are called kings and our God is the King of kings. In Bible times as well as in ancient lands where kings reigned, a lesser king never appeared before a greater king empty handed. This is a principle also for the kingdom of God. He is the King of kings and we are kings. To appear before Him without an offering is to not fully understand who we are and how to appear before this King of kings. When the Queen of Sheba came before Solomon, she came with gift. However there is a principle that establishes that when you come with gifts, you should not go empty-handed. On receiving the lesser king's gift, the greater king must bless the lesser king with a more valuable gift.

And king Solomon gave unto the queen of Sheba all her desire, whatsoever she asked, beside that which Solomon gave her of his royal bounty. So she turned and went to her own country, she and her servants. 1 Kings 10:13

The freewill offering is what you bring to God to appreciate His good hand on our life and His favour that has been manifesting in the things you do.

Freewill offerings are what you bring to establish fellowship with God.

The freewill offering is what determines the inflow of blessings after the tithe has opened the windows.

The offering establishes fellowship with the King of kings, it is freewill and one is not called to do more than he can, however, there are times when it must be a sacrifice, because the kingdom of God requires it.

Take ye from among you an offering unto the LORD: whosoever is of a willing heart, let him bring it, an offering of the LORD; gold, and silver, and brass, Exodus 35:5

And it came to pass after these things, that God did tempt Abraham, and said unto him, Abraham: and he said, Behold, here I am. And he said, Take now thy son, thine only son Isaac, whom thou lovest, and get thee into the land of Moriah; and offer him there for a burnt offering upon one of the mountains which I will tell thee of. Genesis 22:1-2

And the king said unto Araunah, Nay; but I will surely buy it of thee at a price: neither will I offer burnt offerings unto the

LORD my God of that which doth cost me nothing. So David bought the threshingfloor and the oxen for fifty shekels of silver. 2 Samuel 24:24

God laid claim to Isaac and Abraham knew he had no other choice but to lay him on the altar. He laid Isaac on the altar knowing that whatever followed would be a hundred fold return, like Jesus also taught.

And every one that hath forsaken houses, or brethren, or sisters, or father, or mother, or wife, or children, or lands, for my name's sake, shall receive an hundredfold, and shall inherit everlasting life. Matthew 19:29

However when we worship God with our offering, we negate the power of the seed sown when we complain or act as if God owes us and must return quickly what was proportionate to the seed we had sown. God will certainly bless the believer, but it is an offering of worship, and it must truly die at the altar.

Giving to the Poor

In another chapter we will be talking extensively about the poor, however, the scriptures teach us to give to the poor. We give to the poor to continue our act of benevolence and to be a blessing to others as taught by scriptures.

So I took the chief of your tribes, wise men, and known, and made them heads over you, captains over thousands, and captains over hundreds, and captains over fifties, and captains over tens, and officers among your tribes. Deuteronomy 1:15

Scriptures are very clear; you either fall under the category of a person in need of supply or a supplier of the needs.

He that hath pity upon the poor lendeth unto the LORD; and that which he hath given will he pay him again. Proverbs 19:17

This passage which we have read supports the statement of the Lord Jesus Christ when He said, "When we give a cup of water to one of the poor, we have done it as to the Lord." When we release what God has provided for us we bring healing to the hurting and become an extension of the kingdom of God.

Giving to the poor becomes an instrument of deliverance from every yoke and danger.

Blessed is he that considereth the poor: the LORD will deliver him in time of trouble. The LORD will preserve him, and keep him alive; and he shall be blessed upon the earth: and thou wilt not deliver him unto the will of his enemies. Psalm 41:1-2

The plan of the enemy is the destruction of the poor, but such a plan is foiled because you have chosen to be an instrument of blessing to the poor. David is an example of a man who gave to the poor. When Ziklag was invaded and his family, property and that of his soldiers was carried away by an invading army, David's ability to provide for a hungry Egyptian by the roadside was instrumental to the discovery of what was stolen from him.

When you give to the poor it is not necessarily in order that the anointing upon the poor will release any blessing or favour upon you. But certainly the liberality of your soul provokes the grace of God to cause an increase in your life.

There is that scattereth, and yet increaseth; and there is that withholdeth more than is meet, but it tendeth to poverty. The liberal soul shall be made fat: and he that watereth shall be watered also himself.   Proverbs 11:24-25

When the increase comes by reason of blessing the poor, it is also not for you to hoard, but to be able to use in touching more lives.

2. The vow or pledges

A vow is a pledge, a commitment made by you to serve the Lord with a special offering, either prior or after a breakthrough.

A vow often would be what you have chosen before the Lord to do in response to a call to carry out a project or because of a vision you have on your heart. Once a vow is made before the Lord it is binding upon the person who made the vow.

Thy vows are upon me, O God: I will render praises unto thee. Psalm 56:12

A vow is a covenant which we have made to the Lord and God therefore holds us responsible for the words we have spoken.

God is good and the level of His goodness is determined by how good His Word is. And because He is good, He expects us to be good with our words.

Our vows reveal our commitment to our worship of God.

Vow, and pay unto the LORD your God: let all that be round

*about him bring presents unto him that ought to be feared.
Psalm 76:11*

It is a form of worship we have chosen ourselves and therefore the fulfilment becomes important.

It is a snare to the man who devoureth that which is holy, and after vows to make enquiry. Proverbs 20:25

It is important to learn that a commitment has been made once you have made a vow. It would have been better if it were not made, so having made it, fulfilment becomes necessary.

When thou vowest a vow unto God, defer not to pay it; for he hath no pleasure in fools: pay that which thou hast vowed. Better is it that thou shouldest not vow, than that thou shouldest vow and not pay. Ecclesiastes 5:4-5

Once the vow is made and the believer makes the commitment, God also is committed to you to answer whatever prayer or decree you put forth before Him; He is committed to making them happen.

Thou shalt make thy prayer unto him, and he shall hear thee, and thou shalt pay thy vows. Thou shalt also decree a thing, and it shallbe established unto thee: and the light shall shine upon thy ways. Job 22:27-28

Remember the vow is sometimes used as a method of advancing the kingdom of God as we make pledges towards projects.

HOW TO FULFIL THE STEWARDSHIP OF GIVING

God wants us to continue to worship Him with that which He has provided in our giving and not only should we continue but we should increase our levels of giving. However, it must be done with the right spirit and in the right way. It must be done with love. For it to be without love, giving becomes legalism.

And though I bestow all my goods to feed the poor, and though I give my body to be burned, and have not charity, it profiteth me nothing.

It must be motivated by our desire to please Him and to be a blessing to other people.

And the king said unto Araunah, Nay; but I will surely buy it of thee at a price: neither will I offer burnt offerings unto the LORD my God of that which doth cost me nothing. So David bought the threshingfloor and the oxen for fifty shekels of silver. 2 Samuel 24:24

And walk in love, as Christ also hath loved us, and hath given himself for us an offering and a sacrifice to God for a sweetsmelling savour. Ephesians 5:2

It is not the level of giving alone that is important; it is the attitude of the giver that is paramount.

Honour the LORD with thy substance, and with the firstfruits of all thine increase: Proverbs 3:9

This in effect means that our offerings stay on earth while our attitude is what God receives. That is why therefore the scriptures teach us not to give grudgingly (2 Corinthians 9:7); out of compulsion (2 Corinthians 9:7); but cheerfully (2 Corinthians 9:7); generously (2 Corinthians 9:5); bountifully (2 Corinthians 9:6); purposefully (2 Corinthians 9:7); abundantly (2 Corinthians 9:8); liberally (2 Corinthians 9:11,13).

But this I say, He which soweth sparingly shall reap also sparingly; and he which soweth bountifully shall reap also bountifully. Every man according as he purposeth in his heart, so let him give; not grudgingly, or of necessity: for God loveth a cheerful giver. And God is able to make all grace abound toward you; that ye, always having all sufficiency in all things, may abound to every good work: 2 Corinthians 9:6-8

Being enriched in every thing to all bountifulness, which causeth through us thanksgiving to God. Whiles by the experiment of this ministration they glorify God for your professed subjection unto the gospel of Christ, and for your liberal distribution unto them, and unto all men; 2 Corinthians 9:11,13

When giving is done outside of a heart of love, generosity and cheerfulness, the purpose is defeated and the blessing is hindered.

Giving should be planned.

Upon the first day of the week let every one of you lay by him in store, as God hath prospered him, that there be no gatherings when I come. 1 Corinthians 16:2

Paul in writing to the Corinthians said they should gather all that they were going to give before he came. This means in effect that the haphazard giving of believers, whereby it is as if there were caught unawares on Sunday morning, also reflects what they should expect in the realm of the spirit. So nothing precludes you from praying every January on what your level of offering should be each year, or to pray before you go to a meeting as to what you should give to the Lord.

Recognise also that the quality and quantity of your seed determines the quality and quantity of your harvest. Bear in mind that once you set the percentage or level of giving, you have already fixed the level of blessing that will flow to you. Sowing generously produces reaping generously.

> *Give, and it shall be given unto you; good measure, pressed down, and shaken together, and running over, shall men give into your bosom. For with the same measure that ye mete withal it shall be measured to you again. Luke 6:38*

In the same vein the person who sows sparingly will have produced back to him a sparing or limited harvest.

Give under all circumstances; do not wait until it is comfortable and convenient to give. The person who has learnt to give in times of challenges and has been consistent with giving will experience the continuous supply of God. Giving to the Lord must always be with a heart that responds to whatever the Lord tells you to do. For example, God fixed the tithe and obedience to it must be 100 per cent.

Certainly God never wants a person to go beyond their ability in the giving of their offering. It is no use giving and jeopardising the happiness of the giver, but make sure that you never come before the Lord empty handed. You cannot replace the act of giving with fasting, praying or prophesying. Though they are good Christian actions they do not replace the act of covenant that is expressed in giving.

> *Every man according as he purposeth in his heart, so let him give; not grudgingly, or of necessity: for God loveth a cheerful giver. 2 Corinthians 9:7*

It should not be done haphazardly as we said earlier on, but rather as person investing in the kingdom of heaven. When the tabernacle of God was to be built in the wilderness, Moses knew the people had the gold, yet he asked that whatever giving was to be done must be done willingly.

Take ye from among you an offering unto the LORD: whosoever is of a willing heart, let him bring it, an offering of the LORD; gold, and silver, and brass, Exodus 35:5

Never give in the atmosphere of grudge or force, rather with excitement in order to know the blessings that would follow.

That also helps you so that if there was a delay in the manifestation of your blessing, it does not stop your ability to celebrate the goodness of God.

Never give out of a corrupt heart, if there is a sin problem, ensure that you have repented and moved on.

And when ye stand praying, forgive, if ye have ought against any: that your Father also which is in heaven may forgive you your trespasses. Mark 11:25

Never give an offering that will make your family go through financial difficulties or cause anyone to grumble.

The act of obedience must be matched by the act of recognising the importance of you rejoicing in the step you have taken.

WHY PEOPLE DO NOT GIVE

People do not give because of their lack of knowledge.

If you are ignorant of what God said concerning giving, you will hold back because your nature says to do so. People do not give because of their ignorance of their covenant rights and blessings that follows giving by the believer. People do not give because of their lack of understanding of the responsibility of the believer in being part of the perpetuation of the gospel.

How then shall they call on him in whom they have not believed? and how shall they believe in him of whom they have not heard? and how shall they hear without a preacher? And how shall they preach, except they be sent? as it is written, How beautiful are the feet of them that preach the gospel of peace, and bring glad tidings of good things! But they have not all obeyed the gospel. For Esaias saith, Lord, who hath believed our report? So then faith cometh by hearing, and hearing by the word of God. Romans 10:14-17

Some other people do not give because they express fear. They are afraid that God might not do what He promised.

For all the promises of God in him are yea, and in him Amen, unto the glory of God by us. 2 Corinthians 1:20

Some are afraid that as they tithe or release their offering it might not work for their increase; however God is not a man that He should lie.

God is not a man, that he should lie; neither the son of man, that he should repent: hath he said, and shall he not do it? or hath he spoken, and shall he not make it good? Numbers 23:19

Fear also makes people want to give from what they control, unknown to them that it is not until they release it that they can know how God can increase it. Some others are afraid because they look at the mitigating circumstances, the situations in which they are, and refuse to give.

He that observeth the wind shall not sow; and he that regardeth the clouds shall not reap. As thou knowest not what is the way of the spirit, nor how the bones do grow in the womb of her that is with child: even so thou knowest not the works of God who maketh all. In the morning sow thy seed, and in the evening withhold not thine hand: for thou knowest not whether shall prosper, either this or that, or whether they both shall be alike good. Ecclesiastes 11:4-6

Selfishness is a major reason why many stop short of giving or worshipping God with their tithes and offering. The innate nature of man says, "Keep it to yourself, why release it." The innate nature of man says, "Do it yourself." However that ends up in closing the windows of heaven, and the worse thing is to try and operate under a closed heaven. The innate nature of man, the selfish nature of man causes people to miss a major opportunity to act like Jesus and be givers. He was the Ultimate Giver.

However, if anything has been major in stopping people from giving towards the kingdom it is deception that is brought by the culture around us. This culture would say that preachers are the ones grabbing our money and therefore we should keep it to ourselves. This is a knee-jerk reaction and shortsighted because a man has no power to hinder your blessing once the seed from your hand has been released.

There are also religious lies that can hold a person down, lies we tell ourselves like, "the poorer the better". We misconstrue scriptures and say things to the effect that,

"Maybe rich men won't go to heaven." We dealt with this under 'The Mindset'.

THE CONSEQUENCE OF NOT GIVING

We have established that one of the key reasons God wants us to give is for the establishment and promotion of His kingdom. The greatest consequence of not giving to God is financial barrenness. This is what we will look at in more detail.

Whenever there is financial barrenness, there is always a missing element that needs to be put in perspective. To lack financially is a challenge, but to be financially barren is even tougher.

Causes of financial barrenness would be:

1. The unwillingness primarily to build the kingdom of God

Thus speaketh the LORD of hosts, saying, This people say, The time is not come, the time that the LORD'S house should be built. Haggai 1:2

The people in the book of Haggai had rejoiced at their deliverance from Babylonian captivity and possibly promised a vow to rebuild His temple, but no sooner did they get to the land than they forgot the vows they made.

2. The neglect of the things of the Lord

Is it time for you, O ye, to dwell in your cieled houses, and this house lie waste? Haggai 1:4

3. Preference for one's personal security to the well-being of the ministry and the things of God

Ye looked for much, and, lo, it came to little; and when ye brought it home, I did blow upon it. Why? saith the LORD of hosts. Because of mine house that is waste, and ye run every man unto his own house. Haggai 1:9

Jesus told the story of the rich man whose focus was upon himself. He was so selfish that he did not realise why God brings the blessing. The blessing was to touch the world, not just for personal gain. Those who are unable to make kingdom investments would not know kingdom enjoyment. Those who do not know kingdom addiction would not experience supernatural addition. Such people become very busy building an empire for themselves.

The people in the book of Haggai withheld their tithes and all their other givings. When the tithe is withheld the curse is released on whatever is left. When there is a curse on what you have, hard work cannot break the cycle of defeat.

Ye are cursed with a curse: for ye have robbed me, even this whole nation. Malachi 3:9

The consequences of financial barrenness

Solomon said one of the things that is never satisfied is a womb that has never borne a child.

The horseleach hath two daughters, crying, Give, give. There are three things that are never satisfied, yea, four things say not, It is enough: The grave; and the barren womb; the earth that is not filled with water; and the fire that saith not, It is enough. Proverbs 30:15-16

When you go through financial barrenness, you work hard and have no fruit to show.

1. There will be poor results

Ye have sown much, and bring in little; ye eat, but ye have not enough; ye drink, but ye are not filled with drink; ye clothe you, but there is none warm; and he that earneth wages earneth wages to put it into a bag with holes. Haggai 1:6

2. Unsatisfied desire

A man under the curse of financial barrenness keeps pursuing and never meets his target. Such a person has a deep hunger but his thirst and hunger is never satisfied. Financial barrenness is a life that is more like chasing a shadow and never meeting up. Financial barrenness brings physical brokenness. Sickness and disease follow disobedience in the act of withholding the tithe and the offering. It follows when financial barrenness is manifested.

3. Social degradation

Ye have sown much, and bring in little; ye eat, but ye have not enough; ye drink, but ye are not filled with drink; ye clothe you, but there is none warm; and he that earneth wages earneth wages to put it into a bag with holes. Haggai 1:6

When a man walks in disobedience he becomes socially degraded. They wear clothes but they are never warm. In other words a life of embarrassment and shame becomes the portion of a man who has withheld what he ought to have used to serve the Lord.

Social degradation is the portion of the man that is under the scourge of financial barrenness. So when God said He would deliver His people from shame, a disobedient Christian has just exposed himself to what he should have been delivered from.

4. Economic wastage

Unsolicited bills, contingencies that are not planned for, indulgences that cannot be broken from are the things that follow. When monies are withheld from God, particularly the tithe, God will collect it back and that with 20 per cent interest.

One of the ways it is collected back is by the shutting down of things in the life of the disobedient.

5. Shattered dreams

God said they would look for much but indeed it would come to little. Dreams will not match realities. The hopes of a financially barren person will be shattered, inflation follows, the nation, the people, families who refuse to honour God will find things inflated all around them. There will be more, but they are only able to buy less.

6. Domestic problems

Family arguments, marital problems follow where there is financial barrenness. Eighty-five per cent of family troubles in the modern world are centred around finance. Either the lack of it or in some cases much abundance becomes the reason for family fights. Where the family has learnt to honour the Lord, the little they have is with the peace of God. Contentment follows the other supplies they have.

7. Short-lived victory

If they had any victory at all, the heavens withhold the dew.

Therefore the heaven over you is stayed from dew, and the earth is stayed from her fruit. Haggai 1:10

8. Perpetual lack

A man is under financial barrenness when heaven withholds its blessings. The man operates under a closed heaven, and to be under a closed heaven means prayers are not answered, and heaven is like brass. Wherever the man who has the heavens closed over him turns, things do not work, rather things are difficult.

Flying over a desert like the Sahara in Africa, all you can see is brown land, because the place has not known rain or moisture in many years. The same effect rests upon the life of a man who is under financial barrenness. This is more than lack; he is barren, not bearing fruit. There is a lot of activity but no fruit.

9. Withdrawal of God's approval

Therefore the heaven over you is stayed from dew, and the earth is stayed from her fruit. Haggai 1:10

When the approval of heaven is withdrawn from a man, he is like the rebellious that dwell in deserts, who makes his gathering with scorpions and desert foxes.

God setteth the solitary in families: he bringeth out those which are bound with chains: but the rebellious dwell in a dry land. Psalm 68:6

10. Absence of divine blessing

When the heaven withholds its dew, it is symbolic of spiritual dryness. When heaven withholds its blessing, the inner man rots, beautiful things become ugly, businesses collapse, children go wayward, people depend on past glory and repetition. Their lives become deflated; devourers come and break down all that the man has built.

And I will restore to you the years that the locust hath eaten, the cankerworm, and the caterpiller, and the palmerworm, my great army which I sent among you. Joel 2:25

Long hours of work do not present evidence of any blessing.

I returned, and saw under the sun, that the race is not to the swift, nor the battle to the strong, neither yet bread to the wise, nor yet riches to men of understanding, nor yet favour to men of skill; but time and chance happeneth to them all. Ecclesiastes 9:11

Works that blossom become represented by mere dust.

11. Divine sanctions

And I called for a drought upon the land, and upon the mountains, and upon the corn, and upon the new wine, and upon the oil, and upon that which the ground bringeth forth, and upon men, and upon cattle, and upon all the labour of the hands. Haggai 1:11

Consequently everything is withheld and whatever remains has dried up. The rain falls elsewhere but not on the land of the man who is under financial barrenness.

And also I have withholden the rain from you, when there were yet three months to the harvest: and I caused it to rain upon one city, and caused it not to rain upon another city: one piece was rained upon, and the piece whereupon it rained not withered. So two or three cities wandered unto one city, to drink water; but they were not satisfied: yet have ye not returned unto me, saith the LORD. Amos 4:7-8

When there is a divine sanction, devourers take over such a life.

I have smitten you with blasting and mildew: when your gardens and your vineyards and your fig trees and your olive trees increased, the palmerworm devoured them: yet have ye not returned unto me, saith the LORD. Amos 4:9

Nations of the earth have known sanctions from the United Nations and at such times things are hard, but imagine when it is a divine sanction. With such upon Israel, their grain was affected; there was no new wine, which is symbolic of joy. No oil, which is symbolic of the anointing. The cattle died which is symbolic of bad investments and bad returns. The labour of their hands went sour which meant physical death. Lives became deflated. In like manner those under divine sanctions experience something similar.

Financial barrenness means barely surviving, scanty crops; it makes a person to be struggling, trying to survive when he should have an abundant life.

Therefore the heaven over you is stayed from dew, and the earth is stayed from her fruit. Haggai 1:10

The thief cometh not, but for to steal, and to kill, and to destroy: I am come that they might have life, and that they might have it more abundantly. John 10:10

12. Poor returns and depleted savings

Is the seed yet in the barn? yea, as yet the vine, and the fig tree, and the pomegranate, and the olive tree, hath not brought forth: from this day will I bless you. Haggai 2:19

13. Economic ruin

And I called for a drought upon the land, and upon the mountains, and upon the corn, and upon the new wine, and upon the oil, and upon that which the ground bringeth forth, and upon men, and upon cattle, and upon all the labour of the hands. Haggai 1:11

When favour is withdrawn and heaven is closed, the atmosphere of financial barrenness prevails. God ceases to smile on His people because the tithe is withheld, the offering is not given and His work suffers neglect. Under these circumstances the people refuse to fulfil the vows they made in His presence. Sowing into the life of a man of God does not provoke the anointing on a man of God and the poor are not blessed or helped. Economic ruin becomes inevitable.

14. Phantom pregnancy

Like as a woman with child, that draweth near the time of her delivery, is in pain, and crieth out in her pangs; so have we been in thy sight, O LORD. We have been with child, we have been in pain, we have as it were brought forth wind; we have not wrought any deliverance in the earth; neither have the inhabitants of the world fallen. Isaiah 26:17-18

The worst consequence of financial barrenness is to carry a dream and give birth to nothing. It is to carry a picture, an idea, or a vision, to work so hard and have no result, no fruit to show for it. The word here for wind also means anger, wrath or temper. In other words when vision is unfulfilled, when dreams do not happen because of disobedience, one becomes quick-tempered, angry at God, man and everything because of the dreams that do not match the reality of life. It also means to be "despondent, to be breathless."

THE CURE FOR FINANCIAL BARRENNESS

Obviously from this chapter, the cure for financial barrenness is to go back to giving. However before there is a giving, there must be repentance because God deserves to be fully obeyed, not partially. God deserves to be revered, respected, venerated and honoured above all gods.

Thus saith the LORD of hosts; Consider your ways. Haggai 1:7

Then Zerubbabel the son of Shealtiel, and Joshua the son of Josedech, the high priest, with all the remnant of the people, obeyed the voice of the LORD their God, and the words of Haggai the prophet, as the LORD their God had sent him, and the people did fear before the LORD. Haggai 1:12

The believer must learn to walk by God's instruction, not by   people's opinion. Haggai came back after the seventh month with a word from the Lord, challenging the people that truly there will be change if they learn to serve Him.

The Word of God is with us and in our hands today. As we read it we must obey. The tithe must not be given only in moments of convenience, but one must recognise that it is a command that produces a commanded blessing.

As the dew of Hermon, and as the dew that descended upon the mountains of Zion: for there the LORD commanded the blessing, even life for evermore. Psalm 133:3

We must now follow our repentance with an expectant heart. Expectation is necessary for experience.

Who is left among you that saw this house in her first glory? and how do ye see it now? is it not in your eyes in comparison of it as nothing? Haggai 2:3

Be strong

Yet now be strong, O Zerubbabel, saith the LORD; and be strong, O Joshua, son of Josedech, the high priest; and be strong, all ye people of the land, saith the LORD, and work: for I am with you, saith the LORD of hosts: Haggai 2:4

Because it has been bad in the past does not mean that it will always be.

Be led by the Lord

Yet now be strong, O Zerubbabel, saith the LORD; and be strong, O Joshua, son of Josedech, the high priest; and be strong, all ye people of the land, saith the LORD, and work: for I am with you, saith the LORD of hosts: Haggai 2:4

Circumstances must not lead the believer when it comes to the stewardship of giving. Neither should what our friends think or say. For many people it is not their friends or circumstances, but their spouse. If you are married to a person who is unsaved you would need to walk in a lot of wisdom when it comes to the bringing of the tithe to the storehouse, and therefore if you have to pray and wait for the right moment. However, if both are believers, they are obliged to serve the Lord with that which He has provided for them, submitting to God, as the Lord of all things is necessary to make progress.

Be bold

According to the word that I covenanted with you when ye came out of Egypt, so my spirit remaineth among you: fear ye not. Haggai 2:5

Fear is a thief of the blessing of God. Fear will seize the breath in your spirit and make you panic. It will stop you from maximising and reaching your highest fulfilment in life. Boldness is necessary to be able to release what God has provided for us. Boldness is also necessary for you to go in and take what God has already prepared for you. God wants you to prosper and no devil can stop you.

WHEN YOU REPENT AND WALK IN OBEDIENCE, WHEN YOU REVERE GOD FOR WHO HE IS, THE RESULT OF COURSE WILL BE:

1. Divine visitation

And I will shake all nations, and the desire of all nations shall come: and I will fill this house with glory, saith the LORD of hosts. Haggai 2:7

2. Glory will be restored back into your finances and every area of your life

And I will shake all nations, and the desire of all nations shall come: and I will fill this house with glory, saith the LORD of hosts. Haggai 2:7

Nothing is as tough as a life without glory; nothing is as empty as a life that does not know the glory of the Lord.

And the glory of the LORD shall be revealed, and all flesh shall see it together: for the mouth of the LORD hath spoken it. Isaiah 40:5

3. Financial breakthrough will follow you

The silver is mine, and the gold is mine, saith the LORD of hosts. Haggai 2:8

God says that all silver and gold belongs to Him; so do not let the devil talk you out of your blessing. Have no apologies for desiring to be blessed, after all it belongs to your Father and it is His work you want to use it for. Satan owns nothing that is why the scripture calls him a thief.

The thief cometh not, but for to steal, and to kill, and to destroy: John 10:10

Whatever he has was stolen from believers who do not know their authority and dominion rights. God made the silver and the gold when He laid the foundation of the earth. We are yet to come into the greatest blessing God has for His people because they are the ones He will use for the propagation of His Word in these last days.

4. There will be abundant peace

The glory of this latter house shall be greater than of the former, saith the LORD of hosts: and in this place will I give peace, saith the LORD of hosts. Haggai 2:9

Once obedience is put in place, the revelation of the blessing of God will far exceed the troubles you have seen.

It is safe to say whether it is the tithe, offering, vows or blessing the poor, giving is living. God has not left room for questions when it comes to obeying Him either in the tithe or in serving Him with our offering. When He called Abraham, *"Get thee out,"* Abraham did not say, "Where and why am I going?" The Bible says, *"So Abraham departed."*

When you get excited about obeying God, God will be happy to lift you and promote you beyond imagination.

Praise ye the LORD. Blessed is the man that feareth the LORD, that delighteth greatly in his commandments. Wealth and riches shall be in his house: and his righteousness endureth for ever. Psalm 112:1,3

As we serve the Lord with that which He has provided for us, let us do it with a heart of purity.

> O LORD our God, all this store that we have prepared to build thee an house for thine holy name cometh of thine hand, and is all thine own. I know also, my God, that thou triest the heart, and hast pleasure in uprightness. As for me, in the uprightness of mine heart I have willingly offered all these things: and now have I seen with joy thy people, which are present here, to offer willingly unto thee. O LORD God of Abraham, Isaac, and of Israel, our fathers, keep this for ever in the imagination of the thoughts of the heart of thy people, and prepare their heart unto thee: 1 Chronicles 29:16-18

Let us recognise and elevate the lordship of the Lord Jesus Christ in everything we do, so that we will see in our hands a harvest. Enjoy the blessing God is bringing as His favour that flows from Him. He is our Father from whom all blessings flow. Obey God in giving and worship Him with that which He provides.

Every New Year make it a habit to think of starting the year with a new level of giving. That certainly will bring you into a new level of receiving. Be free with your giving, never let giving look like a burden to you. Make it a faith step. Rejoice at the opportunity to serve God with the substance He has provided. Always remember you will never achieve your full potential unless you are free to release what is in your hand. It is when you release what is in your hand that you can receive what is in God's hand.

Obedience is crucial. It cannot be belittled, or put aside. It is only those who are willing and obedient that will eat the best of the land.

If ye be willing and obedient, ye shall eat the good of the land: Isaiah 1:19

Intimacy is paramount; it is your acquaintance with God that will bring you into His gold.

Acquaint now thyself with him, and be at peace: thereby good shall come unto thee. Then shalt thou lay up gold as dust, and the gold of Ophir as the stones of the brooks. Job 22:21, 24

Covenant blessing and breakthrough is not provoked by chance, but by obedience.

Bringing The Firstfruit to God

There are many Christians who honestly worship God with their offerings and their tithe and still wonder why they struggle. Some have become a victim of a poverty mentality. They have difficulty breaking from the cycle of financial defeat and financial hardship.

May I quickly draw your attention to Proverbs 3:9,10

Honour the LORD with thy substance, and with the firstfruits of all thine increase: So shall thy barns be filled with plenty, and thy presses shall burst out with new wine. Prov. 3:9-10

In verse nine the word "firstfruit" pops out and many times this has been interpreted as the tithe, whereas it is what it describes itself to be. The challenge given by Solomon to honour God with the firstfruit of our increase, after we have used the capital provided to start a business.

Honor the Lord with your capital and sufficiency [from righteous labors] and with the firstfruits of all your income; Proverbs 3:9 (Amplified)

The result is told us in verse ten (Amplified) that our barns will be loaded with plenty.

So shall your storage places be filled with plenty, and your vats shall be overflowing with new wine. Proverbs 3:10 (Amplified)

However we can notice that many serve the Lord of plenty but are having a barn house that is empty and their life is a matter of barely getting along. Something is not right somewhere and if we look carefully it is tied to the obedience or disobedience to the principle of the firstfruit. The firstfruit connects you to plenty.

For if the firstfruit be holy, the lump is also holy: and if the root be holy, so are the branches. Romans 11:16

What you do with the firstfruit determines what happens to the rest. It is called the principle of the first. The first determines the last. The firstfruit and the tithe are different from each other. The tithe is mentioned 32 times in scripture and incidentally the first fruit is also mentioned 32 times. The firstfruit comes up in the Bible before the tithe is mentioned.

And Abel, he also brought of the firstlings of his flock and of the fat thereof. And the LORD had respect unto Abel and to his offering: Genesis 4:4

The tithe is not discussed in scriptures until Genesis. The firstfruit means the first one, not the last one.

For whatsoever things were written aforetime were written for our learning, that we through patience and comfort of the scriptures might have hope. Romans 15:4

God told Moses that He would have to possess the first of everything that belonged to Israel.

And it shall be when the LORD shall bring thee into the land of the Canaanites, as he sware unto thee and to thy fathers, and shall give it thee, Exodus 13:11

WHY, YOU MAY ASK?

According to Exodus 13:14, it was because God brought out Israel as His firstfruit out of Egypt, the place of bondage. And while they were in Egypt the firstborn of every man and every beast in Egypt died, yet within the camp of Israel, despite their being in bondage, being broke and battered, their firstborn was reserved. With such a visual and graphic illustration of God's ability to deliver, in Him protecting the first born of people who were considered as slaves, He taught Israel to remember the experience in Egypt and to perpetuate it in subsequent generations.

And the LORD spake unto Moses, saying, Speak unto the children of Israel, and say unto them, When ye be come into the land which I give unto you, and shall reap the harvest thereof, then ye shall bring a sheaf of the firstfruits of your harvest unto the priest: And he shall wave the sheaf before the LORD, to be accepted for you: on the morrow after the sabbath the priest shall wave it. Leviticus 23:9-11

And ye shall eat neither bread, nor parched corn, nor green ears, until the selfsame day that ye have brought an offering unto your God: it shall be a statute for ever throughout your generations in all your dwellings. Leviticus 23:14

And the feast of harvest, the firstfruits of thy labours, which thou hast sown in the field: and the feast of in gathering, which is in the end of the year, when thou hast gathered in thy labours out of the field. Exodus 23:16

God taught them that they should celebrate the bringing in of the firstfruit.

And the feast of harvest, the firstfruits of thy labours, which thou hast sown in the field: and the feast of ingathering, which is in the end of the year, when thou hast gathered in thy labours out of the field. Exodus 23:16

It should be done for the whole world to see.

Only the firstling of the beasts, which should be the LORD'S firstling, no man shall sanctify it; whether it be ox, or sheep: it is the LORD'S. And all the tithe of the land, whether of the seed of the land, or of the fruit of the tree, is the LORD'S: it is holy unto the LORD. He shall not search whether it be good or bad, neither shall he change it: and if he change it at all, then both it and the change thereof shall be holy; it shall not be redeemed. Leviticus 27:26, 30,33

Verse 27 in particular shows that what God wants is the best. He wants the right and He wants the mature. It is the first thing, the first best which comes into the hand of the believer that should be given to God. Verse 30 and verse 33 show clearly that this has nothing to do with the tithe, it is a separate kind of giving for worship.

The tithe of everything is fixed, you cannot change the tithe, but according to verse 33 of Leviticus chapter 27, you can give the best firstfruit to God.

In Bible times firstborn animals belonged to Him. Whoever obeyed Him in the principle of the firstborn had the respect of God. In the plagues of Egypt, the firstborn of the Egyptians died, the firstborn of the Israelites lived. If an Egyptian did it right, if he offered his firstborn to God or sacrifice to God, his firstborn lived, while an Israelite who did it wrong, his firstborn would have died.

For us today it is the first of whatever comes into our hand from business, salary, a raise or a promotion. It is the first from a new job, if the first is blessed, the lump will be blessed. If the first is unblessed the whole lump will be unblessed. This principle undergirds the reason why God demanded that Jericho be left alone for Him. Jericho was the first city they conquered and therefore it belonged to God; nothing could be taken from Jericho but to be burnt as a hallowed offering to God. Achan could not take his eyes off the nice things, the beautiful things in Jericho and therefore he touched what had been set aside as a hallowed thing for God.

WHERE DO YOU SEND YOUR FIRSTFRUIT?

The principle of the firstfruit has been obscure in the Body of Christ for quite a long time and therefore whenever a new revelation is made clear it is challenging to some people. That in effect does not stop it from being a principle taught by the Word of God. In Bible times people brought the firstfruit to the prophet over their life. Why? Because your prosperity is in the hand of your prophet; ask the widow whose husband died.

> Now there cried a certain woman of the wives of the sons of the prophets unto Elisha, saying, Thy servant my husband is dead; and thou knowest that thy servant did fear the LORD: and the creditor is come to take unto him my two sons to be bondmen. And Elisha said unto her, What shall I do for thee? tell me, what hast thou in the house? And she said, Thine handmaid hath not any thing in the house, save a pot of oil. Then he said, Go, borrow thee vessels abroad of all thy

neighbours, even empty vessels; borrow not a few. And when thou art come in, thou shalt shut the door upon thee and upon thy sons, and shalt pour out into all those vessels, and thou shalt set aside that which is full. So she went from him, and shut the door upon her and upon her sons, who brought the vessels to her; and she poured out. And it came to pass, when the vessels were full, that she said unto her son, Bring me yet a vessel. And he said unto her, There is not a vessel more. And the oil stayed. Then she came and told the man of God. And he said, Go, sell the oil, and pay thy debt, and live thou and thy children of the rest. 2 Kings 4:1-7

Your healing is in the hand of your prophet. 2 Kings 5:1-14

Your favour is in the hand of your prophet.

Now Hannah, she spake in her heart; only her lips moved, but her voice was not heard: therefore Eli thought she had been drunken. And Eli said unto her, How long wilt thou be drunken? put away thy wine from thee. And Hannah answered and said, No, my lord, I am a woman of a sorrowful spirit: I have drunk neither wine nor strong drink, but have poured out my soul before the LORD. Count not thine handmaid for a daughter of Belial: for out of the abundance of my complaint and grief have I spoken hitherto. Then Eli answered and said, Go in peace: and the God of Israel grant thee thy petition that thou hast asked of him. And she said, Let thine handmaid find grace in thy sight. So the woman went her way, and did eat, and her countenance was no more sad. 1 Samuel 1:13-18

The widow of Zarephath offered her first meal to Elijah and her family never lacked. Saul offered a seed to Samuel when he was looking for his father's donkey. Naaman brought his seed for the man of God in order to also experience the healing of God.

What you are seeking remains lost until you recognise the power of your connection to the prophet over your life. It is that connection that makes divine impartation possible. It is that connection that prepares you for all that God has for you. So you must stay connected and prepare yourself for impartation.

The prophet or priest over you also has responsibility to you. He does not have access to your firstfruit unless his ministry is producing in your life.

And the LORD said unto Aaron, Thou and thy sons and thy father's house with thee shall bear the iniquity of the sanctuary: and thou and thy sons with thee shall bear the iniquity of your priesthood. Numbers 18:1

And the LORD spake unto Aaron, Behold, I also have given thee the charge of mine heave offerings of all the hallowed things of the children of Israel; unto thee have I given them by reason of the anointing, and to thy sons, by an ordinance for ever. This shall be thine of the most holy things, reserved from the fire: every oblation of theirs, every meat offering of theirs, and every sin offering of theirs, and every trespass offering of theirs, which they shall render unto me, shall be most holy for thee and for thy sons. In the most holy place shalt thou eat it; every male shall eat it: it shall be holy unto thee. And this is thine; the heave offering of their gift, with all the wave offerings of the children of Israel: I have given them unto thee, and to thy sons and to thy daughters with thee, by a statute for ever: every one that is clean in thy house shall eat of it. Numbers 18:8-11

The scriptures would only teach us to give the firstfruit from increase. So if there is no increase there is no giving. The believer must recognise that their deliverance is in the hand of a man of God. When people faced financial challenges in Bible times, they were not referred to just a financial counsellor, they went to a man of God. When people faced the ravages of death in Bible times, the hospital was not enough; they went to a man of God.

Certain teachings may be hated by the devil because it is the final frontier of what will bring you out of bondage. When we look through the scriptures, we see that every time God will unleash a blessing on a people or a nation He has always used the man of God. The man of God is a gift to you to bring you out of bondage and to bring you into God's blessing.

And by a prophet the LORD brought Israel out of Egypt, and by a prophet was he preserved. Hosea 12:13

And the first of all the firstfruits of all things, and every oblation of all, of every sort of your oblations, shall be the priest's: ye shall also give unto the priest the first of your dough, that he may cause the blessing to rest in thine house. Ezekiel 44:30

The widow of Zarephath was under a clear instruction in 1 Kings 17, so she did not come out of bondage by accident, she did not escape death by accident, supernatural provision did not happen by accident. She was commanded to give the firstfruit to a servant of God, she was told not to be afraid, because there is a tendency to begin to imagine how the cake that goes out of one hand becomes multiplied in coming back. This principle has nothing to do with the way a man of God feels or how you feel, it is a principle that must be obeyed in order for the release to follow.

God also gave His Son as the firstfruit of the resurrection.

But now is Christ risen from the dead, and become the firstfruits of them that slept. 1 Corinthians 15:20

God believes in it and if it is good enough for God, it should be good enough for you. If the first one got up, others will get up, so

God knew that principle and applied it, His firstborn got up, and when we die we shall get up and be changed at His appearance.

Once the principle of the firstfruit is obeyed, God will change your status. God will break the power and grip of poverty and lack. The firstfruit will cause the blessing to come upon you and by the blessing we mean God empowering you to prosper.

The book of Ezekiel 44:30 gives us an insight on the result of obedience when it comes to bringing the firstfruit.

And the first of all the firstfruits of all things, and every oblation of all, of every sort of your oblations, shall be the priest's: ye shall also give unto the priest the first of your dough, that he may cause the blessing to rest in thine house. Ezekiel 44:30

The status of the believer will change because he has obeyed God in the first fruit. God will break the power and grip of selfishness, and not that alone, the power and grip of every negative; poverty, lack, sickness, woes, shame, tragedy, bereavements, calamities and all that are not mentioned here. Their power will be broken. Not only is the power of the negative broken, the uncommon blessing of God is released upon the believer.

God's uncommon blessing includes financial increase, physical promotion and the apparent manifestation of the goodness of God. Bringing the firstfruit is like the action of the little boy in the story of the ministry of Jesus who released his two pieces of fish and a loaf of bread, the young man's lunch pack meant that 12 men followed him with baskets full of breakthrough and prosperity. Because he released his lunch pack first, he got what God had for him.

Every time we give with a spirit of worship and a sense of understanding of the power of the firstfruit, God brings us into an experience of the plenty. When we let go of what we have we become 'goal-getters.'

Sometimes the release of the firstfruit may be tearful, but the result will be cheerful. As you sow the seed into a place where you see things happening, new things will begin to happen for you. Firstfruit in its real sense is a sweet smelling savour that pleasures God. The attitude, commitment, that makes a man release his first salary, first increment or profit makes such a person a candidate for receiving a greater favour from God. The release of the firstfruit is a sign of love towards God. It is an indication of the desire to please God with our seed; it is an act of worship that is ultimate and committing in its price. Primarily in scriptures, the release of firstfruit is towards prophets. Jesus tells us what happens when we release our seed and bless His prophets; the ministers who have sown into our lives.

He that receiveth a prophet in the name of a prophet shall receive a prophet's reward; and he that receiveth a righteous man in the name of a righteous man shall receive a righteous man's reward. Matthew 10:41

So my friend, it is time for us to walk into the zone of obedience that we may have the fullness of all that God has for us.

If ye be willing and obedient, ye shall eat the good of the land: Isaiah 1:19

It is in the area of our releasing what we have through obedience that makes us to walk in the God-kind of blessing.

I have shewed you all things, how that so labouring ye ought to support the weak, and to remember the words of the Lord Jesus, how he said, It is more blessed to give than to receive. Acts 20:35

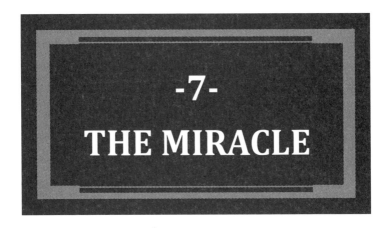

-7-
THE MIRACLE

The state of our finances matters to God. It is of such importance that He has already scheduled a way out of every financial crisis we are likely to face. God is not One to watch His children shed tears without taking notice of the reason and making a way out. There surely is a way out. It just is a matter of finding it. Every prison has a door. Rivers have bridges over them, and for every mountain there might be a tunnel. However, it is not enough to have a means of escape, it is important to find it.

When people fall into hard times, the first thing they do is to find how to get out of the pit or the hollow they have fallen into. A common occurrence in the scripture is God supplying miracle money to get His people out of financial situations. Miraculous financial supply however, does not mean that needs will not arise again.

That is a reason why mindsets will need to be corrected and methods for making money will need to be discovered. All through the scriptures, when God rescued His people from financial battles, He would not send them to financial consultants but to prophets. If we must come into our wealthy place, we must experience the place of a prophet in our life.

> *And by a prophet the LORD brought Israel out of Egypt, and by a prophet was he preserved. Hosea 12:13*

Why would God use a prophet for miraculous financial deliverance? I believe it is because often times such people have tasted failure and therefore qualify to be our mentors for breakthrough. So it is no use staying in the mess of financial difficulty listening to people who only fuel your doubts and unbelief. It is no use discussing your financial trouble with those who you call your relations who are probably not financially better off.

What is the use of discussing your trouble with a man who is on the same mutual road of financial difficulty with you? What is the use listening to voices that have no solution? After all, the voices you listen to become the voices you understand and believe. The picture you see is the picture you will believe. Ten spies infected the whole of Israel with the picture of impossibility, doubt and unbelief because that was what they also saw. They painted the same picture before millions, and millions preferred an evil report. What you talk about increases, what you meditate on becomes bigger and anything you give verbal and visual attention to will increase.

HOW TO EXPERIENCE MIRACULOUS SUPPLY

It is important to pursue the people God is using to fuel your faith - the prophet in your life who unlocks your faith and makes you believe God. These pursuits might be paying an extra price, you will have to show that you recognise the mantle of God upon their life and treasure it. The pursuit of a man of God to experience a miraculous financial supply in our days may be by listening to their tapes or reading their books in order to come into the degree of revelation they share.

On a day when ten spies stood before the children of Israel and painted a picture of gloom, there was Caleb and Joshua who said in spite of the giants, "We are well able". You need to discern the Joshuas and Calebs around you who by the prophetic word of their mouth starve your doubts and feed your faith. They speak victory instead of the size of the giants of financial need. Faith is necessary to come in before you can see results.

So then faith cometh by hearing, and hearing by the word of God. Romans 10:17

Sit down and listen, absorb what will make your faith and finances grow. You must recognise that when you need deliverance in your finances, the way God has scheduled victory is by sending a man of God to you. If you recognise that anointing the chains will fall off you. Let us take a close look at seven instances in scripture when people experienced a miraculous supply.

Case no.1 - The widow of Zarephath

And she said, As the LORD thy God liveth, I have not a cake, but an handful of meal in a barrel, and a little oil in a cruse: and, behold, I am gathering two sticks, that I may go in and dress it for me and my son, that we may eat it, and die. And Elijah said unto her, Fear not; go and do as thou hast said: but make me thereof a little cake first, and bring it unto me, and after make for thee and for thy son. For thus saith the LORD God of Israel, The barrel of meal shall not waste, neither shall the cruse of oil fail, until the day that the LORD sendeth rain upon the earth. And she went and did according to the saying of Elijah: and she, and he, and her house, did eat many days. 1 Kings 17:12-15

We are confronted with the story of a woman who has almost everything against her. This was a widow in a male dominated   society. She had a son who was still dependent on her and there were members of her household who were probably too old to be able to take care of themselves. She had one last meal for herself and her son. Hurting, devastated, starving and nearing death she had come to fetch wood to cook the last meal. When the prophet Elijah met her, he did not blame, criticise or cuddle her. Any of this would have either sided with her because of her pain or chided her because she had only one meal and probably had not been working. Elijah did not sympathise with her, he knew how to get her out of trouble.

To be politically correct, Elijah could have given her something in addition to the one meal she had. He would have looked like a good aid worker or a great helper to someone in need. Those who stir up your faith are only getting something to you, not something from you. In order for you to come into what God has for you, there has to be a release of the seed in your hand to experience the supply God has. She listened and discerned that he was a man of God and was willing to follow his instruction regardless of how ridiculous or illogical it seemed.

Case no.2 - The sons of the prophet

And the sons of the prophets said unto Elisha, Behold now, the place where we dwell with thee is too strait for us. Let us go, we pray thee, unto Jordan, and take thence every man a beam, and let us make us a place there, where we may dwell. And he answered, Go ye. And one said, Be content, I pray thee, and go with thy servants. And he answered, I will go. So he went with them. And when they came to Jordan, they cut down wood. But as one was felling a beam, the axe head fell into the water: and he cried, and said, Alas, master! for it was borrowed. And the man of God said, Where fell it? And he shewed him the place. And he cut down a stick, and cast it in thither; and the iron did swim. Therefore said he, take it up to thee. And he put out his hand, and took it. 2 Kings 6:1-7

In Bible times, the axe head was a means of livelihood for whoever owned it. The axe head was the tool a whole family probably depended on to put food on their table and now it had slipped to the bottom of a river. Recovering it was impossible. After all it cannot float. Archimedes law of flotation would argue that for it to float it would have to have a hollow and being iron with just a hole, it certainly would not float. Then comes the miraculous intervention of God and the axe head, which was a debt the sons of the prophets owed, floated and was restored.

Case no.3 - The lepers and the promise of abundance

Then Elisha said, Hear ye the word of the LORD; Thus saith the LORD, To morrow about this time shall a measure of fine flour be sold for a shekel, and two measures of barley for a shekel, in the gate of Samaria. Then a lord on whose hand the king leaned answered the man of God, and said, Behold, if the LORD would make windows in heaven, might this thing be? And he said, Behold, thou shalt see it with thine eyes, but shalt not eat thereof. And there were four leprous men at the entering in of the gate: and they said one to another, Why sit we here until we die? If we say, We will enter into the city, then the famine is in the city, and we shall die there: and if we sit still here, we die also. Now therefore come, and let us fall unto the host of the Syrians: if they save us alive, we shall live; and if they kill us, we shall but die. And they rose up in the twilight, to go unto the camp of the Syrians: and when they were come to the uttermost part of the camp of Syria, behold, there was no man there. For the Lord had made the host of the Syrians to hear a noise of chariots, and a noise of horses, even the noise of a great host: and they said one to another, Lo, the king of Israel hath hired against us the kings of the Hittites, and the kings of the Egyptians, to come upon us. Wherefore they arose and fled in the twilight, and left their tents, and their horses, and their asses, even the camp as it was, and fled for their life. And when these lepers came to the uttermost part of the camp, they went into one tent, and did eat and drink, and carried thence silver, and gold, and raiment, and went and hid it; and came again, and entered into another tent, and carried thence also, and went and hid it. Then they said one to another, We do not well: this day is a day of good tidings, and we hold our peace: if we tarry till the morning light, some mischief will come upon us: now therefore come, that we may go and tell the king's household. 2 Kings 7:1-9

Israel was going through a period of intense famine. In the previous chapter, it was so bad that people became cannibals. It was at such a time of lack, drought and famine that God used His prophet to speak forth that there would be super-abundance in the space of 24 hours. A supply which was unimaginable since there was nothing growing anywhere in the neighbourhood, let alone it being harvested and distributed. God supernaturally intervened by using the mere shuffling of lepers to reach the ears of a mighty army and scatter them. So Israel had a miraculous supply.

Case no. 4 - The man of Baalshalisha

And there came a man from Baalshalisha, and brought the man of God bread of the firstfruits, twenty loaves of barley, and full ears of corn in the husk thereof. And he said, Give unto the people, that they may eat. And his servitor said, What, should I set this before an hundred men? He said again, Give the people, that they may eat: for thus saith the LORD, They shall eat, and shall leave thereof. So he set it before them, and they did eat, and left thereof, according to the word of the LORD. 2 Kings 4:42-44

This was an Old Testament account of a miracle similar to the one Jesus performed. The bread and grain available were not enough to supply the hundreds of people who were meeting the man of God. It was one man's supply and there were a hundred mouths to feed. When it was time for it to be distributed, the Word of the Lord said, "Give it to the people that they may eat, for thus saith the Lord, they shall eat and have some leftover," and truly it happened according to the Word of the Lord. This is another case of the miraculous supply of God.

Case no.5 - The widow with the pot of oil

Now there cried a certain woman of the wives of the sons of the prophets unto Elisha, saying, Thy servant my husband is dead; and thou knowest that thy servant did fear the LORD: and the creditor is come to take unto him my two sons to be bondmen. And Elisha said unto her, What shall I do for thee? tell me, what hast thou in the house? And she said, Thine handmaid hath not any thing in the house, save a pot of oil. Then he said, Go, borrow thee vessels abroad of all thy neighbours, even empty vessels; borrow not a few. And when thou art come in, thou shalt shut the door upon thee and upon thy sons, and shalt pour out into all those vessels, and thou shalt set aside that which is full. So she went from him, and shut the door upon her and upon her sons, who brought the vessels to her; and she poured out. And it came to pass, when the vessels were full, that she said unto her son, Bring me yet a vessel. And he said unto her, There is not a vessel more. And the oil stayed. Then she came and told the man of God. And he said, Go, sell the oil, and pay thy debt, and live thou and thy children of the rest. 2 Kings 4:1-7

This is one of the bad cases of bankruptcy in Bible times. A widow, two sons, nothing in the house, everything possibly taken over by bailiffs, leaving the family with a bottle of oil which they thought was insignificant and therefore unnecessary. The widow turned to the prophet. She knew where to go when she was in trouble, not to a financial consultant or someone to reschedule her debt. She listened to the prophet and released what was in her hand in order to receive what was in God's hand. The prophet again did not pity them or side with their trouble. He did not cuddle them but provoked them to release what was in their hand. The miraculous is always released by the act of the person in the situation, and leaving God to turn the ridiculous to the miraculous.

Case no.6 - Saul and the lost donkeys

And he said unto him, Behold now, there is in this city a man of God, and he is an honourable man; all that he saith cometh surely to pass: now let us go thither; peradventure he can shew us our way that we should go. Then said Saul to his servant, But, behold, if we go, what shall we bring the man? for the bread is spent in our vessels, and there is not a present to bring to the man of God: what have we? And the servant answered Saul again, and said, Behold, I have here at hand the fourth part of a shekel of silver: that will I give to the man of God, to tell us our way. 1 Samuel 9:6-8

Saul and his servant were troubled because of what they had lost. They had searched all day and could not find the donkeys. The donkeys were their source of income. Saul's father was presented as a wealthy man in scriptures. The donkeys were his tools of trade. The problem persisted until they remembered the man of God. Saul's servant recognised the power of an offering that once it is released, it brings you into the experience of the miraculous. He brought the seed of the offering to the prophet of God. In the providence of God the seed Saul's servant brought provoked more than what he came to recover. It launched Saul into his destiny as the first monarch of the nation of Israel.

Case no.7 - Peter's Inland Revenue bill

And when they were come to Capernaum, they that received tribute money came to Peter, and said, Doth not your master pay tribute? He saith, Yes. And when he was come into the house, Jesus prevented him, saying, What thinkest thou, Simon? of whom do the kings of the earth take custom or tribute? of their own children, or of strangers? Peter saith unto him, Of strangers. Jesus saith unto him, Then are the children free.Notwithstanding, lest we should offend them, go thou to the sea, and cast an hook, and take up the fish that first cometh up; and when thou hast opened his mouth, thou shalt find a piece of money: that take, and give unto them for me and thee. Matthew 17:24-27

Peter was confronted with the need to pay his tax. Having followed the Nazarene these three years, he needed a miracle. Peter turned to the prophet in his life, the Lord Jesus Christ. The Lord in turn told him to do what seemed ridiculous but which produced the miraculous. Miracle money is possible if we learn to talk to God. There is a key to the treasure house of life if we would stop scratching for little things. Your responsibility is to find that key and obey the instructions of God.

If ye be willing and obedient, ye shall eat the good of the land: Isaiah 1:19

If they obey and serve him, they shall spend their days in prosperity, and their years in pleasures. Job 36:11

Prophets do not come with the title of financial consultant. As a matter of fact, the appearance of John the

Baptist was such that people just had to tolerate that God was with him. Sometimes God's best gifts arrive in paper bags. Man looks on the outward but God looks on the inward appearance. The scriptures cannot be broken that if we believe His prophets, we will prosper.

And they rose early in the morning, and went forth into the wilderness of Tekoa: and as they went forth, Jehoshaphat stood and said, Hear me, O Judah, and ye inhabitants of Jerusalem; Believe in the LORD your God, so shall ye be established; believe his prophets, so shall ye prosper. 2 Chronicles 20:20

Recognise Your Appointed Place

Miraculous finance is possible if we first of all recognise our appointed place.

And there was a famine in the land, beside the first famine that was in the days of Abraham. And Isaac went unto Abimelech king of the Philistines unto Gerar. And the LORD appeared unto him, and said, Go not down into Egypt; dwell in the land which I shall tell thee of: Sojourn in this land, and I will be with thee, and will bless thee; for unto thee, and unto thy seed, I will give all these countries, and I will perform the oath which I sware unto Abraham thy father; And I will make thy seed to multiply as the stars of heaven, and will give unto thy seed all these countries; and in thy seed shall all the nations of the earth be blessed; Because that Abraham obeyed my voice, and kept my charge, my commandments, my statutes, and my laws. Genesis 26:1-5

Then Isaac sowed in that land, and received in the same year an hundredfold: and the LORD blessed him. And the man waxed great, and went forward, and grew until he became very great: For he had possession of flocks, and possession of herds, and great store of servants: and the Philistines envied him. For all the wells which his father's servants had digged in the days of Abraham his father, the Philistines had stopped them, and filled them with earth. And Abimelech said unto Isaac, Go from us; for thou art much mightier than we. And Isaac departed thence, and pitched his tent in the valley of Gerar, and dwelt there. And Isaac digged again the wells of water, which they had digged in the days of Abraham his father; for the Philistines had stopped them after the death of Abraham: and he called their names after the names by which his father had called them. Genesis 26:12-18

Where you are matters to God. Where you are must not be determined by the mass movement of people but the leading of God. To experience miraculous supply you have to be where He wants you to be. God told Elijah to go to the brook Cherith, the place of God's ordination in the time of famine for the supply of Elijah's need.

Get thee hence, and turn thee eastward, and hide thyself by the brook Cherith, that is before Jordan. 1 Kings 17:3

Later He told him to go to Zarephath because that was the next place God had ordained a person to be a blessing to Elijah. Where you are determines what grows within you. Where you are determines what you see. If you stay long where God has said 'bye bye' you miss the next season of God.

Ye have compassed this mountain long enough: turn you northward. Deuteronomy 2:3

Jesus recognised the importance of being at the right place.

And he must needs go through Samaria. John 4:4

You cannot receive the favours scheduled for a geographical place if you are not there. Joseph had to be in Egypt to be able to stand before Pharaoh. Ruth had to be in Israel to be able to meet Boaz. The daughter of Pharaoh was by the riverside at the appointed time for the miraculous encounter of picking up Moses. God gave Abraham a specific instruction to go to a land He had chosen.

Now the LORD had said unto Abram, Get thee out of thy country, and from thy kindred, and from thy father's house, unto a land that I will shew thee: And I will make of thee a great nation, and I will bless thee, and make thy name great; and thou shalt be a blessing: And I will bless them that bless thee, and curse him that curseth thee: and in thee shall all families of the earth be blessed. Genesis 12:1-3

The appointed place is connected to the miracle of God's financial supply, find it and be there. Jesus gave 500 people instructions to tarry for the Holy Spirit. One hundred and twenty people took Him seriously. They were the only ones who experienced the full package of the outpouring of the Spirit. There are various places in scripture: there is a place of no blessing, there is a place of some blessing and there is a place of much blessing. However, there is a place of much more than enough.

For thus saith the LORD, Behold, I will extend peace to her like a river, and the glory of the Gentiles like a flowing stream: then shall ye suck, ye shall be borne upon her sides, and be dandled upon her knees Isaiah 66:12

Thou hast caused men to ride over our heads; we went through fire and through water: but thou broughtest us out into a wealthy place. Psalm 66:12

You must recognise anointed people.

We have seen earlier instances where God used the office of a prophet to make the outpouring of the miraculous supply possible. Anointed people have an assignment to destroy yokes, remove burdens and to release joy.

And it shall come to pass in that day, that his burden shall be taken away from off thy shoulder, and his yoke from off thy neck, and the yoke shall be destroyed because of the anointing. Isaiah 10:27

Coming into a miraculous supply requires that you recognise who carries the anointing around you. It is the recognition of that anointing as well as God's ability to supply your need that makes things work even in the midst of adversity.

Sojourn in this land, and I will be with thee, and will bless thee; for unto thee, and unto thy seed, I will give all these countries, and I will perform the oath which I sware unto Abraham thy father; And I will make thy seed to multiply as the stars of heaven, and will give unto thy seed all these countries; and in thy seed shall all the nations of the earth be blessed; Because that Abraham obeyed my voice, and kept my charge, my commandments, my statutes, and my laws. Genesis 26:3-5

Recognise Your Appointed Times

There will be a need for you to recognise your appointed times. The appointed time for blessing may be in the middle of a crisis. Miraculous supply is often at the time when there is a challenge. Some have allowed those challenges to determine their attitude and worship of God with the seed in their hand. They have been intimidated by the difficulties they see. In the moment of pain it is difficult to see how the pain will go. During tough times it is difficult to think straight. Satan likes you to be timid and to run away. During crisis times you must always act contrary to what the enemy expected you to do. Crisis times should become your seed sowing time; that was what Isaac did in the verse we just read. Crisis time is the time to fight back.

Submit yourselves therefore to God. Resist the devil, and he will flee from you. James 4:7

It is a time to recognise that a miracle is about to be born. The atmosphere of battle is the breeding ground for breakthroughs. So crisis must not distort your picture of miraculous supply. The expectation must run high because that is the only magnet that can put you in the net of God's favour. The expectation must provoke you to sow seed in order to come into your harvest. The expectation is a current that brings in your hundred-fold return. The release of expectation is also a release of change.

Recognise The Need to Sow Seed

You must recognise the need to sow seed to provoke miraculous supply.

Famine times are the times God wants to show that He can open the heavens to you, but if you look at the heavens you will not sow seed in the natural. So look to God and hear what He says.

He that observeth the wind shall not sow; and he that regardeth the clouds shall not reap. As thou knowest not what is the way of the spirit, nor how the bones do grow in the womb of her that is with child: even so thou knowest not the works of God who maketh all. In the morning sow thy seed, and in the evening withhold not thine hand: for thou knowest not whether shall prosper, either this or that, or whether they both shall be alike good. Ecclesiastes 11:4-6

The change is scheduled for your appointed seed sowing time. Your vision will only happen at such a time. Miraculous supply and fruitfulness will only manifest at such a time.

And he shall be like a tree planted by the rivers of water, that bringeth forth his fruit in his season; his leaf also shall not wither; and whatsoever he doeth shall prosper. Psalm 1:3

There is a rain scheduled to wet the seed you sow and it is ordained by God in order for you to experience the supply He wants.

Neither say they in their heart, Let us now fear the LORD our God, that giveth rain, both the former and the latter, in his season: he reserveth unto us the appointed weeks of the harvest. Jeremiah 5:24

Miraculous supply means that you recognise God's ability to create your own due season. It may be out of season for other people. Those who know the power of miraculous supply also recognise that God schedules His own season for them. Do not follow the regular.

These wait all upon thee; that thou mayest give them their meat in due season. Psalm 104:27

The eyes of all wait upon thee; and thou givest them their meat in due season. Psalm 145:15

Who then is a faithful and wise servant, whom his lord hath made ruler over his household, to give them meat in due season? Matthew 24:45

Humble yourselves therefore under the mighty hand of God, that he may exalt you in due time: 1 Peter 5:6

You must recognise your appointed seed time and harvest time. Experiencing miraculous financial supply will require training your spirit to sow seed when it seems difficult for the flesh to do so. Your seed time is not always the most convenient; it is probably in the middle of trouble. However, your seed time is necessary because it is whatever wipes away the tears and brings back joy into your life or that of other people. Your seed contains your future, you can abort it or make it abound.

A great harvest begins with a small seed. What is in your hand right now has the capacity to release what has been promised to you. A seed in your hand is the key to the beginning of miracles. There is something in your life, in your hand right now that is supposed to birth something in your future. You must find it and sow it.

The man of God asked the widow with her two sons, "What is in your house?" Firstly, she said nothing until she realised she had a bottle of oil. A seed in your hand is a key to the beginning of miracles. The forgetfulness that the seed in your life is given to you by God makes you to have a problem releasing it to Him. So once you have a problem releasing your seed, you will have a challenge coming into the miraculous supply of God. However, once the release takes place God lets go of what has been stored up for you. On the other hand when you keep what is in your hand you hinder your scheduled breakthrough. When the size of your seed increases, the size of your harvest is magnified.

But this I say, He which soweth sparingly shall reap also sparingly; and he which soweth bountifully shall reap also bountifully. 2 Corinthians 9:6

-8-
THE MAKING

The scripture is true when it says that the love of money is the root of all evil. However the lack of it also is the cause of a lot of troubles. The tentacles of poverty are not only keeping 60 per cent of the world under its grip, the World Bank now describes certain nations as highly indebted and poor countries (HIPC).

These are nations whose gross national product and gross domestic product are not able to relieve them of the challenges they face. In this chapter we first of all want to look at steps to overcoming lack.

The Webster's comprehensive dictionary of the English Language, the Encyclopedic edition, defines lack as, "To be without, to have none or too little of, to be short by, the state of being in need, want, deficiency and failure." This is true indeed because lack makes people feel like a failure. Therefore to overcome lack you would need to:

1. Replace false belief

For as he thinketh in his heart, so is he: Eat and drink, saith he to thee; but his heart is not with thee. Proverbs 23:7

The problem with many people is not that they do not know. However what they know oftentimes is the wrong and it is the reason for their lack. Such misinformation becomes a shaky foundation upon which to build. For example, if you ask some people what they want they will say a good job, a great job, a fantastic job. It is this thought that leads the poor to think that saving your money in some little account is a good investment, unknown to them that is not how real investment is done or major monies are come into.

So in effect what we are saying is that contrary to common belief in society, finding a good job and working hard is not what builds, neither is putting your money into some savings account. Along with this wrong thinking is the false assumption that all debts are wrong. Yes, indebtedness is a bad thing; however there is investment debt that is actually self-made wealth and may provide some degree of leverage. We shall cover this in more detail later.

The thought of some people is not to fail; they are so afraid of failing that they protect themselves. Along with this kind of thought is the feeling that unless you can count wealth in cash, it is not wealth. However, wealth maybe something that is not material; intellectual property is wealth. Have you noticed that when you travel through airports customs check, you get to the point where it asks, "Something to declare" or "Nothing to declare?"

Really they expect you to go through "Nothing to declare," if you do not carry mighty suitcases. However, between your ears may be what is worth millions of pounds.

2. Have a clear vision for life

A man whose journey is not clearly defined is likely to be stopped by every obstacle.

And the LORD answered me, and said, Write the vision, and make it plain upon tables, that he may run that readeth it. For the vision is yet for an appointed time, but at the end it shall speak, and not lie: though it tarry, wait for it; because it will surely come, it will not tarry. Habakkuk 2:2-3

If you plan to take a long trip you need a road map to determine the best route. Locate where you are on that map, relative to where you are going and as the journey begins determine what is of value to you and when your mission, purpose or goal will be established.

Unless you define where you are today, it will be very difficult to know if you are making progress. And where you are today must be defined within the context of where you really want to go.

3. Recognise that there is a job, business or vocation near you

It is locked up waiting for you.

For where your treasure is, there will your heart be also. Matthew 6:21

And I will give thee the treasures of darkness, and hidden riches of secret places, that thou mayest know that I, the LORD, which call thee by thy name, am the God of Israel. Isaiah 45:3

Prior to writing this book, a young man came to see me in one of my counselling sessions. He studied accountancy, however he works as a manager in a residential house for elderly people. He has a passion for the elderly, but has never thought about the fact that one of the areas where most governments invest money into and are looking for good people to manage are residential homes for the elderly. He had a job seeker mentality though surrounded by people who were already into that business.

4. Make yourself a lifetime student of the Word

Study to shew thyself approved unto God, a workman that needeth not to be ashamed, rightly dividing the word of truth. 2 Timothy 2:15

In May 2003 I was speaking in Zimbabwe sharing 80 principles on finance as presented in the book of Proverbs. A man who owned a bank and had been a believer for years, walked up to me to say that he never knew that the Book of Proverbs had so much to reveal on finance.

A good man leaveth an inheritance to his children's children: and the wealth of the sinner is laid up for the just. Proverbs 13:22

5. You cannot wait until you have a lump sum before you start the process of investing

It must be a habit formed from the days when you made a little money. The one time governor of the Central Bank of the country of Nigeria, Dr Clement Isong said that a person who cannot save in the day of £1, will not be able to save when he earns £1,000.

6. Do not spend what you do not have

It is like reaping where you did not sow. If you must use

credit, it must be in order to make more money, not in a downward investment. That is using money in a way that does not bring any returns, but only increases liability.

7. Live below expectation

Let your conversation be without covetousness; and be content with such things as ye have: for he hath said, I will never leave thee, nor forsake thee. Hebrews 13:5

The Bible says your conduct should be without covetousness. A man who has the intent to make money must recognise the fact that he would not need to confirm the expectation of certain people, or to show that he has money. Delayed gratification is a proof of maturity and the opposite is also true.

8. Determine your hourly rate

It is very easy for one to look at his gross salary and announce it to the world. However, imagine a man who lives in the United Kingdom and earns £25,000 annually. To him it sounds like a good sum. Yet such a man must recognise that with direct and indirect tax, as well as National Insurance, 40 per cent of that money is deducted from his income, leaving him with 60 per cent. As a committed Christian and a believer, 10 per cent should go to the Lord in the tithe, leaving the believer with 50 per cent.

The £12,500 left of the £25,000 must now be divided by 2,000 which is the annual number of hours we work. This leaves the individual with £6.25 per hour.

To a person who reads this book in a third world situation, it sounds like a lot of money, however, while you have £6,25 per hour, you must recognise that your fridge does not wait for you, it continues to consume electricity. Your car guzzles gas, every waking moment, means you are spending.

If you do not like how much your hourly rate comes to after you have done all these deductions, you must increase the value of what you do with each hour, in order for you to come into the kind of finances you want to have.

9. Learn to receive God's instruction and what He says

A wise man will hear, and will increase learning; and a man of understanding shall attain unto wise counsels: Proverbs 1:5

The advantage the believer has compared to the general public is the fact that we have the opportunity to be instructed by God.

And thine ears shall hear a word behind thee, saying, This is the way, walk ye in it, when ye turn to the right hand, and when ye turn to the left. Isaiah 30:21

10. Recognise the deposit of God in your life

By this I mean there are certain skills you have, that you must find and hone. Identify these skills, particularly the skills that are consistent with the key result areas of your life. Failure to do a skills inventory will mean that people might short-change you, under pay you, over-use you and under value you. Your key skill areas must be the ones in which you are very good, in order to earn the kind of money you desire.

Your weakest key skills preset the standard you could ever rise to because you are only as strong as your greatest weakness. That sounds like an oxymoron, but that is the truth. A great army is only as strong as its weakest member.

11. Learn from others

It is impossible to change unless you are ready to draw from other people to make yourself a better person. The area in which you are ignorant is the area where you perpetually pay the price.

UNDERSTANDING BIBLICAL PROSPERITY

We said earlier that true wealth is not only in your ability to count the cash. Biblical prosperity has seven kinds of manifestation.

1. Spiritual prosperity

And this is life eternal, that they might know thee the only true God, and Jesus Christ, whom thou hast sent. John 17:3

And be not drunk with wine, wherein is excess; but be filled with the Spirit; Ephesians 5:18

It is the state of being where your spirit is fully nourished and you are enjoying your relationship with the Lord Jesus Christ.

2. Mental prosperity

For God hath not given us the spirit of fear; but of power, and of love, and of a sound mind. 2 Timothy 1:7

Thou wilt keep him in perfect peace, whose mind is stayed on thee: because he trusteth in thee. Isaiah 26:3

To be mentally prosperous is to have a sense of security, tranquillity and peace. It is not to be ruffled by the things around you, but rather to have your confidence in God.

3. Intellectual prosperity

As for these four children, God gave them knowledge and skill in all learning and wisdom: and Daniel had understanding in all visions and dreams. Daniel 1:17

This is an area in which the future lies. The next great revolution is in the area of intellectual prosperity. You need insight, insight to know what to do in your chosen field of endeavour. Insight to know those who possess knowledge in the particular area of your endeavour. It is the ability to protect the knowledge you have and to get ready to pay whatever price it requires to make the intellectual property which God will give you, the divine insight, the creativity, something worth buying.

4. Physical health and healing

Health is wealth. He who has life has hope, but more so when you have divine health flowing from God to you, irrespective of immediate circumstances, then you are a blessed person.

Beloved, I wish above all things that thou mayest prosper and be in health, even as thy soul prospereth. 3 John 1:2

And said, If thou wilt diligently hearken to the voice of the LORD thy God, and wilt do that which is right in his sight, and wilt give ear to his commandments, and keep all his statutes, I will put none of these diseases upon thee, which I have brought upon the Egyptians: for I am the LORD that healeth thee. Exodus 15:26

5. Relational prosperity

It takes one person to introduce you to some favours. Somebody once said, "You are only four references away from whoever you want to meet." Certain relationships are not worth the input and investment. They divide you, dilute your vision, distract your focus, dominate your intellect and destroy your confidence.

6. Financial prosperity

For ye know the grace of our Lord Jesus Christ, that, though he was rich, yet for your sakes he became poor, that ye through his poverty might be rich. 2 Corinthians 8:9

And God is able to make all grace abound toward you; that ye, always having all sufficiency in all things, may abound to every good work: 2 Corinthians 9:8

This is the crux of our teaching in this book. It is God's desire that His people prosper and know progress in everything they do.

Beloved, I wish above all things that thou mayest prosper and be in health, even as thy soul prospereth. 3 John 1:2

It delights God to see His servants prosper.

Let them shout for joy, and be glad, that favour my righteous cause: yea, let them say continually, Let the LORD be magnified, which hath pleasure in the prosperity of his servant. Psalm 35:27

7. Family prosperity

Of all the areas in which a man must make progress, it is important to recognise that biblical prosperity is not complete unless you know family prosperity.

Lo, children are an heritage of the LORD: and the fruit of the womb is his reward. As arrows are in the hand of a mighty man; so are children of the youth. Happy is the man that hath his quiver full of them: they shall not be ashamed, but they shall speak with the enemies in the gate. Psalm 127:3-5

Children, obey your parents in the Lord: for this is right. Honour thy father and mother; (which is the first commandment with promise;) That it may be well with thee, and thou mayest live long on the earth. Ephesians 6:1-3

It is no use having everything and no one to enjoy it with you.

HOW TO RECEIVE BIBLICAL PROSPERITY

1. Recognise the law of sowing and reaping

It is an unbreakable law that what a man sows is what he reaps. If you send out noise, you will reap an echo.

But this I say, He which soweth sparingly shall reap also sparingly; and he which soweth bountifully shall reap also bountifully. Every man according as he purposeth in his heart, so let him give; not grudgingly, or of necessity: for God loveth a cheerful giver. 2 Corinthians 9:6-7

While the earth remaineth, seedtime and harvest, and cold and heat, and summer and winter, and day and night shall not cease. Genesis 8:22

If you look up to God for biblical prosperity, you must also recognise that it flows to those who have learnt the power of sowing. However, the totality of the teachings under the 10 Ms of money must be applied. It is not enough to apply certain principles of prosperity without the other aspects.

2. Obey the principle of tithing

Bring ye all the tithes into the storehouse, that there may be meat in mine house, and prove me now herewith, saith the LORD of hosts, if I will not open you the windows of heaven, and pour you out a blessing, that there shall not be room enough to receive it. And I will rebuke the devourer for your sakes, and he shall not destroy the fruits of your ground; neither shall your vine cast her fruit before the time in the field, saith the LORD of hosts. Malachi 3:10-11

3. Give cheerfully

Every man according as he purposeth in his heart, so let him give; not grudgingly, or of necessity: for God loveth a cheerful giver. 2 Corinthians 9:7

4. Give according to your ability

Every man shall give as he is able, according to the blessing of the LORD thy God which he hath given thee. Deuteronomy 16:17

God will never demand from a man to sow a seed he does not have. The giving may be a sacrificial one, yet God will not owe any man.

5. Walk in obedience

If ye be willing and obedient, ye shall eat the good of the land: Isaiah 1:19

If they obey and serve him, they shall spend their days in prosperity, and their years in pleasures. Job 36:11

It is important to recognise that while it is good to sow your seed and bring your offering to the Lord, God expects the walk of obedience to honour Him.

6. Prioritise kingdom business

But seek ye first the kingdom of God, and his righteousness; and all these things shall be added unto you. Matthew 6:33

7. Live in line with the Word of God

Blessed is the man that walketh not in the counsel of the ungodly, nor standeth in the way of sinners, nor sitteth in the seat of the scornful. But his delight is in the law of the LORD; and in his law doth he meditate day and night. And he shall be like a tree planted by the rivers of water, that bringeth forth his fruit in his season; his leaf also shall not wither; and whatsoever he doeth shall prosper. Psalm 1:1-3

8. Believe the promises of God to prosper you

Bring ye all the tithes into the storehouse, that there may be meat in mine house, and prove me now herewith, saith the LORD of hosts, if I will not open you the windows of heaven, and pour you out a blessing, that there shall not be room enough to receive it. And I will rebuke the devourer for your sakes, and he shall not destroy the fruits of your ground; neither shall your vine cast her fruit before the time in the field, saith the LORD of hosts. Malachi 3:10-11

But thou shalt remember the LORD thy God: for it is he that giveth thee power to get wealth, that he may establish his covenant which he sware unto thy fathers, as it is this day. Deuteronomy 8:18

9. Reject and refuse the tendency to be selfish, stingy or cheap

Three times in a year shall all thy males appear before the LORD thy God in the place which he shall choose; in the feast of unleavened bread, and in the feast of weeks, and in the feast of tabernacles: and they shall not appear before the LORD empty: Every man shall give as he is able, according to the blessing of the LORD thy God which he hath given thee. Deuteronomy 16:16-17

10. Look for good ground in which to sow your seed

And these are they which are sown on good ground; such as hear the word, and receive it, and bring forth fruit, some thirtyfold, some sixty, and some an hundred. Mark 4:20

11. Always make God the source of your blessing and the senior partner in your life

And if children, then heirs; heirs of God, and joint-heirs with Christ; if so be that we suffer with him, that we may be also glorified together. Romans 8:17

What then? are we better than they? No, in no wise: for we have before proved both Jews and Gentiles, that they are all under sin; Romans 3:9

12. Let it be clearly established in your life that it is God's will for you to prosper

But without faith it is impossible to please him: for he that cometh to God must believe that he is, and that he is a rewarder of them that diligently seek him. Hebrews 11:6

Beloved, I wish above all things that thou mayest prosper and be in health, even as thy soul prospereth. 3 John 1:2

Once you are between two opinions and doubt the desire of God to bless and increase you, then the prosperity of God eludes.

13. Always follow sound biblical principles as found in the Word of God

Through wisdom is an house builded; and by understanding it is established: And by knowledge shall the chambers be filled with all precious and pleasant riches. Proverbs 24:3-4

I have met a few people who say, "I have given my tithe and brought my offering, why am I not prosperous?" But when you look closely you see that certain principles like hard work, diligence and consistency is found wanting in the things that they do.

14. Make sure at all times you honour the Lord in your method, means and ministry of giving

Honour the LORD with thy substance, and with the firstfruits of all thine increase: Proverbs 3:9

The interesting thing about bringing our seed in offerings and tithes to God is that the money stays on earth for the advancement of His kingdom, but what God gets is our attitude. So God says it is to be done cheerfully, prayerfully and with honour, He sees the attitude.

15. Understand that prosperity is by covenant which cannot be revoked, erased or eradicated

The principle that establishes God's supply to His people is rooted in covenant, a commitment God has made to those who believe Him enough, to supply their needs.

But thou shalt remember the LORD thy God: for it is he that giveth thee power to get wealth, that he may establish his covenant which he sware unto thy fathers, as it is this day. Deuteronomy 8:18

My covenant will I not break, nor alter the thing that is gone out of my lips. Psalm 89:34

Work

Jesus said, *"My Father worketh and hitherto I do."*

But Jesus answered them, My Father worketh hitherto, and I work. John 5:17

He also said furthermore:

I must work the works of him that sent me, while it is day: the night cometh, when no man can work. John 9:4

The scriptures are very strong about the necessity for work. Nothing works like work. Work is the mandate God gave to man from the Garden of Eden until he comes to eternity. The biblical teaching about blessing is that the blessing of the Lord only rests upon the diligent, not the indolent.

He becometh poor that dealeth with a slack hand: but the hand of the diligent maketh rich. Proverbs 10:4

The rich man's wealth is his strong city: the destruction of the poor is their poverty. Proverbs 10:15

He that tilleth his land shall be satisfied with bread: but he that followeth vain persons is void of understanding. Proverbs 12:11

Work is the only thing that produces lasting wealth. The scriptures say the hand of the diligent will rule. So while on one hand we see that God puts the mandate of prosperity upon the believer, yet on another we see that it has to be worked out. Work brings dignity to life. It is the commitment to work that produces lasting wealth.

A good man leaveth an inheritance to his children's children: and the wealth of the sinner is laid up for the just. Proverbs 13:22

The kind of wealth that comes by labour, stays in the house and does not take flight.

Wealth gotten by vanity shall be diminished: but he that gathereth by labour shall increase. Proverbs 13:11

A man who would lead, know promotion and progress, breakthrough and favour must himself be committed to result-producing work, not talk. In the kingdom in which we belong, there is no hiding place for lazy people. God is a worker, Jesus is a worker and the Holy Spirit is a worker. So in effect we are saying that work is your sure way to a perpetual increase.

Wealth gotten by vanity shall be diminished: but he that gathereth by labour shall increase. Proverbs 13:11

Work is that which gives satisfaction to the man who is not lazy.

He that tilleth his land shall be satisfied with bread: but he that followeth vain persons is void of understanding. Proverbs 12:11

The journey to accomplishment is by reason of increase in labour. Work was not meant for punishment, it is God's gift to mankind to discover, develop and deploy all of man's ability.

Every man also to whom God hath given riches and wealth, and hath given him power to eat thereof, and to take his portion, and to rejoice in his labour; this is the gift of God. Ecclesiastes 5:19

Work is what turns your frustration at your lack of fulfilment into what produces. Work is your horse for riding high in life, for crossing the Red Sea that wants to stop you. So in effect do not catch the 'I will do it later' spirit. Come against every sense of procrastination. Work is the investment of time, not the waste of time. If you must make progress with the work of your hand, the 'I know how' attitude must be discarded.

He that covereth his sins shall not prosper: but whoso confesseth and forsaketh them shall have mercy. Prov. 28:13

Work must be strategic and not a little. You must go the extra mile in producing things with excellence.

And whosoever shall compel thee to go a mile, go with him twain. Matthew 5:41

If you do little work, the result will be mediocrity. Let what you do distinguish you; let your work be a mark of distinction. Every man's work is a sign of his capability in life. When you are distinguished in your work, people will know you are dedicated to your cause. Work must also be with quality; when you produce sloppy, substandard, unfinished work, you lose clients, lose face and lose your future. Quality is born through endurance; quality also makes your work endure. Works of quality stand the test of time.

In my book, "101 Great Laws of Success," one of the laws called The Law of Doing says, "Success answers to what positive habit becomes a part of your personality."

In the sweat of thy face shalt thou eat bread, till thou return unto the ground; for out of it wast thou taken: for dust thou art, and unto dust shalt thou return. Genesis 3:19

For we hear that there are some which walk among you disorderly, working not at all, but are busybodies. Now them that are such we command and exhort by our Lord Jesus Christ, that with quietness they work, and eat their own bread. 2 Thessalonians 3:11-12

17 KINDS OF INVESTMENT

1. Leverage

Leverage is an asset you borrow to increase your operational base. Increasing your financial power or advantage by the temporary usage of other assets either borrowed or loaned to increase   effectiveness.

Then he said, Go, borrow thee vessels abroad of all thy neighbours, even empty vessels; borrow not a few. 2 Kings 4:3

The use of leverage in a financial sense is often associated with OPM (other people's money). However, leverage extends beyond other people's money. It could include knowledge, time, credit, etc.

Wherever you can borrow to increase your equity, whatever you can borrow to increase your power to get wealth, when used carefully can help you build and make money. If you are the provider of leverage, it would be wise to watch to whom you make such facilities available. However, you must watch your heart in the process of borrowing, even though it is for investment, because the heart finds it easy to borrow and difficult to pay back.

When taking advantage of leverage, make sure you use it for upward investment. It must not be used to pay for things that do not bring a return. For example, a car.

Be sure that you know the terms, see that it is based on a level you can manage. Do not miss a payment, so as to avoid the fines associated with leverage when you miss payments. Do not confuse anything that is said to be a free of fee payment as being a free of interest payment. Be sure your payments are on time even if you are just paying the minimum amount. Paying on time and not missing a payment actually improves your credit rating.

2. Precious metals and precious gems

And I will give thee the treasures of darkness, and hidden riches of secret places, that thou mayest know that I, the LORD, which call thee by thy name, am the God of Israel. Isaiah 45:3

There is a market for precious metals. After the recent crash in the stock market, investments in gold bars have been on the increase, resulting in an increase in gold price.

3. Savings account

This is the traditional way people understand to deposit their money in accounts held with banks, building societies or savings and loan companies. However, it has its limitations because it is essentially low in interest and easily accessible to the account holder, therefore requiring a lot of discipline for you not to spend the money. It is not exactly a way to see your wealth increase because of the limited interest.

4. Treasury bills

This is a short-term investment paid upon maturation of the bill issued. In the United Kingdom it is a guilt-edge security issued by the British Government. Treasury bills are among the safest of all investments. Backed by the government it is therefore unlikely that the government would default on interest or on repayment of the principles you have invested.

Treasury bills may be short, medium or long-term. In the United Kingdom they are issued in £100 units and can be bought through a stockbroker or a bank.

5. Money market funds

In the United Kingdom the money market is for short-term loans. In the money market money brokers arrange for loans between the banks, the government, the discount houses and the accepting houses. This arrangement is with the Bank of England that acts as the lender of the last resort. It is a method for increasing your income if you have monies in excess of £10,000 you can trade on the money market via a money broker or brokerage house. This will earn you a higher interest than the regular high street bank account or other savings account would have generated for you.

6. Stocks and shares

Stocks and shares are an equity investment; it is the ownership of shares and stocks in a company that is floated on the stock exchange of a country. The dividend received or loss experienced would be determined by the performance of the shares. The prices of shares change constantly; therefore if a company does well then its shares are likely to rise. The prices can fall as well so there is a risk involved. Once you buy stocks and shares in a company, you are technically part of the owners of the company. This means in effect if the shares go up that your money has increased its value through the shares. Dealing in stocks and shares can provide one with leverage.

Investing in the stock market however is one of the most risky investments.

Shares can change your playing field as an individual. You can sell shares through a stockbroker who is authorised to act as your link to the stock market. By registering with a stockbroker you are given a dealing limit with which you can begin to buy and sell shares. For example, you can start in the United Kingdom on the AIM (Alternative Investment Market) where, by starting with penny shares quoted on the AIM, you could use the credit that has been made available to raise some capital for yourself. However, because of the intricacies in dealing with stocks and shares it would be important for you to get educated yourself and to have the time and the ability to follow the performance of your shares.

Some have left the managing of their portfolio to their brokers, who sometimes have had challenges. Therefore it would be important to ensure that you also can watch over your own investment. The beauty of buying shares quoted on any stock exchange, for example the London Stock Exchange, is that you are buying ownership of a small part of a company. You can technically say that you are one of the owners of Sainsbury's Plc or Wal-Mart Plc.

7. Bonds

Bonds are an interest-bearing debt certificate issued either by a financial institution, the government, or companies. It is loaning money to an entity for a defined period or at a specified interest rate. In exchange for your money, you are issued with a certificate of bond that states the interest rate commitment, and the term of payment to you.

8. Commodities market

Commodities are really elements of economic wealth that can be bought or sold. Raw materials can be traded on the commodities market. For example, if you go to the commodities market you are trading in things like grain, coffee, cocoa, wool, cotton, rubber or orange juice. These are sometimes known as soft commodities. There are metals and other solid raw materials that are known as hard commodities and can also be traded on the commodity market.

In this market settlements are usually by a commodity contract. In all these commodities markets you can deal in options and in mutual trust funds. Imagine a situation where you want to invest money but your money is not enough to make an impact. A mutual trust fund is money committed to a portfolio manager who in turn collects from various investors and buys or sells stocks to make profit for you. Monies are gathered from various investors to form the trust.

Unit trusts are special trusts that enable the investors to pull their resources and thereby spread their risk; not only do they spread their risk, they have professional management and a larger sum with which to deal on the market. Unit trusts were made known as self help groups but they are now set up and run by financial companies who create new openings as new markets emerge. A unit trust is one of the tax efficient ways to get your money involved in investments so that the managers can buy and sell within the trust without paying tax. Tax liabilities arise only on dividends and any unit sales by the holder.

9. Retirement funds

We will look at this in more detail under managing money however, pensions fall under this category. By contributing to a pension scheme the employee's contribution attracts tax relief at the maximum highest rate of income tax that they pay within the United Kingdom. The only limit to contributions you can make to your pension fund is you and the maximum allowable by the Inland Revenue. For example your monthly take home income is £1,000. You may chose to pay the highest pension contribution allowed by the Inland Revenue knowing fully well that it is tax-free and that becomes an investment for your future.

10. General businesses

A time to get, and a time to lose; a time to keep, and a time to cast away; Ecclesiastes 3:6

Seest thou a man diligent in his business? he shall stand before kings; he shall not stand before mean men. Proverbs 22:29

In the book of Deuteronomy 28, three phrases tell us the levels of blessing God wants to put on the believer. It says, "Your kneading trough," "your basket," and "your storehouse."

Blessed shall be thy basket and thy store. Deuteronomy 28:5

My understanding is that the kneading trough stands for your pocket, that is your salary. The basket stands for small and medium-sized enterprises (SMEs), while the storehouse stands for major businesses and industries. What you are able to handle and what you are willing to believe God for will determine what you receive. However, it is interesting to notice that from school to selling, there does not seem to be any form of educational system that prepares people for anything more than how to write a CV to get a job. It is like starting as a butterfly and ending up like a cocoon. People are not taught how to create and maintain long-term wealth. They are taught how to get good jobs and manage.

The highest academic degree in business is a Masters in Business Administration. Much of it is not in entrepreneurship; it is in the management of business for others. There is nothing in our school curriculum from the cradle to the grave that teaches a child or an adult anything that is an educational experience in becoming wealthy. Our students go through long years in university without being explicitly taught on how to make wealth.

11. Real estate

There may be many methods for returning a high yield or dividends for people's investments. However, one that I have observed to be a winner of all time is property ownership or real estate. When I came to the United Kingdom in February 1984 I began to minister among the ethnic minorities particularly people of Afro-Caribbean descent. My observation was that apart from a few artisans, masons and other skilled labourers who had come from the Caribbean - who were smart enough to invest in real estate in the 50s and 60s in the United Kingdom when the property market was not as busy - most blacks lived in council apartments. (These are local government owned apartments that were available for rent at a lesser amount.)

Some even celebrated whenever such apartments were allocated to them. Families lived in council apartments for

20 to 25 years and did not see anything wrong with their non-ownership of it. One of the greatest benefits of the Margaret Thatcher era for such people was the 'Right-to-Buy' scheme that was introduced during her tenure as Prime Minister. The lack of sense of ownership and the fact that the rent was low made it attractive.

My family lived for four and a half years in such apartments, from February 1984 to August 1988. Along with the stigma of it being a council apartment also came the squalor, the filth associated with some of it. It is interesting that when the government began to sell and a sense of ownership came upon the people, these same apartments were transformed into unbelievable personal 'castles'. After all, an Englishman's home is his castle.

In the month of August 1988 my family moved into a house which we bought for £65,000. Only £3,250 of this money was ours - the 5 per cent deposit. We were house owners because of other people's money. By 1998, ten years later we paid off the mortgage of this house, though it was really a 25 year mortgage, the house was now worth £100,000. It could have been worth more except for the fact that the interest rate was high at the time we bought. In spite of coming into the property market at such a time, we endured and paid off the mortgage and we now have a house of such high value.

WHY REAL ESTATE?

1. You can recover from mistakes. The house we bought had mice all over the place. It was a first time buyer's experience. However, with such vermin treated and taken care of, the value of the house rose.

2. You can work with other people's money. All that was needed by the bank was good credit and £3,250 (the deposit). A whole house was now ours. The monthly mortgage was just slightly more than our rent in a council apartment. The mortgage market is even better now where you can now buy your first house with no deposit by getting a 100 per cent mortgage.

3. It is easier to multiply your investment. I did not have much knowledge at that time of investment. If I had allowed myself to draw say, £15,000 when the equity of the house rose it could have been the deposit on three other houses which I would have bought and rented out. In the year 2001 I had to buy an apartment by the River Thames in an area known as Essex. Because it was 'buy-to-let' my deposit had to be 20 per cent. At the time of purchase it was £82,000 and my deposit was £16,000. When the building was about to be completed I was notified. I arranged a mortgage and on completion of the building, exchanged and completed the purchase.

The house is now worth £120,000. Look at it this way - the apartment was £82,000 at the time I bought it and my deposit was £16,000. By the time it was ready it was worth approximately £95,000. My £16,000 has now produced an additional £38,000. No bank could ever give you such interest especially over such a short time period.

4. Value can increase with minimal investment. Unless you want the aesthetics of having to live there, some properties will rise in value purely because you touched it up, i.e. you did some repainting or changed the wall paper.

5. Benefits can be drawn through a re-mortgage without selling. Take the illustration of my apartment again, I put a deposit of £16,000, the house is now worth £120,000. My only borrowing was £66,000. This means in effect that the money available to me is approximately £58,000 and that is within a few months of putting a deposit of £16,000 down. I can withdraw the £58,000 and use it for other purposes. I put a tenant in the apartment and their monthly rent just about covered the monthly mortgage repayment.

6. Unlike the stock exchange you do not need to monitor how a property is doing on a minute by minute basis.

7. It is not easily dated. Most investments are dated. Take for example within a week you buy shares today and they may not exist tomorrow. The investment information available on company shares and commodities constantly changes with different things happening around the world. Real estate has every sign of perpetuating. It can be passed down to the great-grandchildren. While shares may be passed down, in one slump of the market it could be wiped out.

8. There are times when there is a slump in real estate, but even at such times it is still relatively better than the other investments at maintaining income.

9. It requires probably less intellectual input compared to the other forms of investment but more leg work. You would need to have intricate details of how the stock market works to be able to participate. You would need to be able to know how to work mutual funds, interest rates and high yield accounts. Most wealthy people keep their wealth in real estate except for a current move by people of Arabian lands to leave their wealth in gold bullions. Generational wealth has always been kept in real estate.

10. Your own money in real estate investment may be a fraction of the total worth. Remember again my number one house, my family investment initially was £3,250 but immediately I had in my hand a house of £65,000. Nobody has ever put such money in your hand in one go because of the nice person you are!

11. Financial institutions are ready to make lines of credit available for real estate, not for the purchase of diamonds, antiques, mutual funds or bond certificates. They are aware that all these may be down and out of the market by just one bad piece of news. However, except for exceptional disasters the property would continue to gain equity, particularly if it is in the right location.

12. It is considered one of the most secure investments you could ever make.

13. Banks hardly give you a loan to invest in shares but cannot wait to give you money if you come to them with a good plan for purchasing real estate.

14. The interest rates on mortgages are always generally lower than business loans. It is interesting that what is likely to give you more profit has lesser interest rates, even where it is a 'buy-to-let.' Most times they only add 1 or 2 per cent above the regular interest rate on residential mortgages.

15. Real estate is attractive to banks because lending can be tied to the very property you are getting a mortgage on.

16. Real estate value does not plummet to the level which shares fall. Hardly will the value of a property be suddenly wiped out except for disasters, earthquakes, hurricanes, tornados or something adverse happening in the neighbourhood where the property is.

17. House prices rise along with their peers. The house I bought and lived in from 1988 to 1998 was a very old house built at the turn of the 20th century. Although it is very old it is in East London. Its proximity to the Stratford tube station in East London - an area which is generating a lot of interest particularly because of European funding. All the properties in the area rose in value, and mine was no exception. On the stock exchange on the other hand, whenever there is a fluctuation in a particular stock it may not necessarily affect other quoted companies.

18. Most investments require a lot of information, education and acquisition of skill in that chosen field. Dealing in the commodities market, or shares and premium bonds require a certain degree of technical expertise, whereas dealing in real estate requires a handful of insight on where to buy, what to buy, when to buy and how to wait for the right deal.

19. Most disasters do not totally wipe away property values and moreover you can insure against such disasters. Most nations and states tend to introduce insurance that takes into account natural disasters that are known for areas of the nation.

20. In the United Kingdom statistics have shown that by the end of the eighth year of setting up companies 80 per cent of such companies fail or fold up. If the same kind of money used in the set up of the company is invested in real estate the property would still be there as long as there are no defaults in the payment of the   mortgage.

21. There is hardly any nation, continent or city where real estate does not do relatively well.

TAKING SMART ACTIONS ON REAL ESTATE

1. Do not pay the standard variable rate for a mortgage - negotiate. Most financial institutions are looking for people to take the mortgage. A quoted rate is not the "law of Medes and Persia" which cannot change.

2. Do not change mortgage lenders if you can save thousands when buying a latter property from the one on which you had a   previous mortgage. It is a matter of asking them to re-schedule the mortgage as you increase your capacity and size of real estate.

3. Despite the penalties attached to a fixed mortgage, find out if by switching to another lender before your fixed term is over you will still pay less monthly payments despite the penalties. Certain building societies/banks have penalties attached to certain mortgage products. Sometimes the value of moving to another lender has greater dividends than the fixed penalty you have to pay. Do not let this threat of payment a penalty stop you from moving.

4. It is no crime to ring your lenders and ask if there is a deal that will save you money. Sometimes lenders have perks and opportunities. However the law out there on some of the opportunities is such that unless you ask you do not know.

5. Go for capped rates without redemption penalties. Certain savings and loans or building societies would offer you a good interest rate and would be willing to cap the rate for a long period of time. However there are still penalties in certain cases if you were to come out before the end of the term. It is better to go for products without redemption penalties.

6. Search for lenders who may want to cover valuation and legal fees, or alternatively who may give a large discount. Certain developers/banks or building societies would be willing to help carry some of your extra costs apart from the initial deposits. They may cover the fees of the specialist surveyor who goes to inspect the house and probably even their legal fees for the transaction. Check it out or ask, there is no harm in asking.

7. Use all available money to reduce your mortgage or buy other houses. Back again to the story of the East London house. When I bought the house for £65,000 I took an endowment mortgage. My knowledge was limited. As a matter of fact the way it was sold to me sounded very interesting. I was made to understand that at the end of 25 years I would own a house and £30,000 cash. However, nobody told me that by the time I would be paying all the mortgage 25 years later, the £30,000 would actually have a real value of £13,000 at the time I would complete the payment.

With further studies and research I came to find that the more I paid the lesser my interest and if I could move it to a repayment mortgage I could pay off on time and be a true owner of the property.

8. Every £100 paid in excess on a fixed monthly payment mortgage equals to £313 or minus two weeks off the total you are supposed to pay. Imagine a mortgage of £600 - if instead of £600 you had paid £700, your £100 over a long period will be equal to paying £313 or rather would take off two weeks from the 25 years of interest rates. Remember you only need to repeat it 26 times to take off a whole year.

HOW TO MANAGE REAL ESTATE

1. Do not insist on investing on properties in your locality out of sentiment. If it becomes necessary to move into another area, go ahead, do it. However, if it will require flying constantly you will need to think carefully about the cost on the long run. You could consider giving it to a managing agent for a small fee.

2. Consider letting out the old house or apartment as you move to the new. Never keep a building empty. Let your money keep working for you while you go to bed.

3. Do not let out your property without informing your mortgagors. They could penalise you if you do not notify them, particularly if the kind of mortgage given to you is residential and not 'buy-to-let'. It is important to be open and honest and let your mortgagors know.

4. Beware of letting agents if you can. A great number of letting agents charge as high as 15 per cent and that is a major chunk of your income. What is wrong with you registering a letting agency?

5. Your insurers will need to know that you are letting out. The insurance on a house to let and a personal residential building may be different. It may attract a higher premium. It is better to pay the premium than to find that you cannot claim.

6. House prices can fall. Stop borrowing all the time on the equity of your house unless it is to create leverage for other investments. You must recognise also that the real estate market is not a 100 per cent safe from price falls. Therefore over-borrowing by the use of the equity of the house could expose you to great dangers.

7. Make sure there is a good demand before you get involved in a 'buy-to-let' deal. However having said that, there is almost no society, city or state where there is not a continuous demand for one or two bedroom apartments.

8. Make higher repayments when you borrow against your home. Higher repayments help to quickly pay off and are a way to create a good exit on the borrowing road.

9. Always compare mortgage rates offered by different institutions.

10. Do not be carried away by interior decoration when buying properties. Check for signs of ageing and of building problems. Do not let the painting fool you from cracks that may not be too obvious, for the signs of settlement, dampness or wormwood.

11. Aim to pay earlier than the number of years on the mortgage.

Owe no man any thing, but to love one another: for he that loveth another hath fulfilled the law. Romans 13:8

12. Except for the situation where you keep using other people's money to create leverage to create more money, it is wiser to see that the mortgage on the immediate house in which you live is cleared.

13. Make efforts to pay before the monthly due date on the mortgage, but whatever you do make sure your payments are always on time.

14. When looking for properties consider the location. It is very important to recognise that the property does not always stand-alone. The environment, the building and the people in the neighbourhood bring down or lift a property.

15. Endeavour to cut down your monthly outlay of payments by having more than the 5 per cent deposit required.

16. Do not go for a leasehold. Only do it if it is an investment property. Leases expire so if you go for a leasehold, ensure that it is a long lease.

17. Check the terms of the contract if it is leasehold so that there are no carry-outs and conditions that make it onerous and impossible to do anything with the property.

18. Check for infestation of ants, rodents and cockroaches. This makes the property hard to sell and it will become a real albatross around your neck.

19. Ensure that there are no covenants or charges on the land. Many times people have bought properties and because they used a cheap solicitor or legal specialist, charges that have been put against the property were not cleared and therefore they find themselves having to pay somebody else's debt.

20. Do not set out to build overseas unless you can supervise the work, and only if it is guaranteed to appreciate. This book might end up in the hands of someone who lives in another nation, e.g. people in the Diaspora. Once you have grown as an adult in your home country, it keeps calling you back, it pulls you and magnetises you. People have inadvertently gone back and built houses, unfortunately, in towns that are too remote for their properties to have any form of equity or value.

21. Do not invest in real estate overseas unless you are going to use it and it should be where properties appreciate.

22. Look for properties that require little work, renovate and sell. If this is done it shows in effect that you are into property investment and you are not doing it for your own residence.

23. If you live overseas be wise with your method of sending money for property purchase. Jesus told the story of the man who went to inspect the land at night and gave it as an excuse for not being able to come to dinner. Inspecting a land at night is an excuse for failure because you cannot quite tell the condition. Buying while you are overseas because you saw a couple of photographs on the Internet may expose you to incredible danger.

24. Always view real estate as an upward investment. Investments are either upward or downward. Downward investment is whatever does not increase the value of your input. Real estate does.

25. Real estate could be a means of generating income without much effort. It just grows with time and with the appreciation of properties in the neighbourhood.

26. Avoid enticing mortgage schemes that have long-term drawbacks. Sometimes people buy part of a property and have shared ownership. While this may give a certain degree of ownership, it exposes you to danger of course.

27. Do not succumb to estate agents languages of pressure. Remember that if you cannot sleep on a decision it may not be worth it.

28. Know other extra costs in the area - property tax, association tax as it is called in America, insurance, land costs and land tax.

29. View your intended property during the daytime so that all is revealed and nothing takes you by surprise after the purchase.

30. Make sure your spouse puts your name on the document of the house in the case where it is a residential property.

31. The crime rate in an area can affect your home and content insurance. It is important to do a demographic survey of the area where you are investing.

32. Ask for a mortgage with daily interest rate calculation. This is necessary because if you pay extra money it reduces the amount of interest that your loan accrues. There are loaning institutions which prefer to do their calculations at the end of the year. This compounds the interest you pay and that works to their advantage and to your disadvantage.

33. If in doubt about the quality of a building, pay for a full structural survey. It is like paying now to avoid a massive problem, it is paying to avoid a nightmare. The cost of ignorance is probably greater than the savings.

34. Survey the building for subsidence or flooding if necessary. Sometimes a property looks nice on the outside but there could be subsidence. Survey properly to ensure no problem comes up later.

35. Avoid co-ownership and housing trusts of associations if you can. It limits your own equity although it gives you an opportunity to start up.

36. The range of local authority services available to you must be checked and verified. Would you have to dispose of your own garbage or is there such a service provided by the local government and how much are you required to pay?

37. Avoid listed buildings unless you are ready for the restrictions. In the United Kingdom there is the listed building system whereby an old building of historical importance will be listed with a grade I , II or III listing. The level of a building's listing determines how much work you can carry out on it without having to get permission.

38. If you are selling remember that every little work carried out will enhance the quality of your property. Just another coat of paint, a few gallons of paint will cost you a couple of hundred pounds but may add thousands to the value.

39. When buying investment properties try for a low deposit mortgage. Imagine a situation where you are buying investment property and you are given 100 per cent mortgage. If those who will rent it are able to pay what covers the monthly outlay, it is a total win for you because it is other people's money creating 100 per cent leverage. Always take out interest only mortgages on your investment properties. This is because you can only offset the interest element when preparing your tax returns.

40. First time buyers should find a mortgage before finding a property.

41. Sign on with agents who have the kind of property you want.

42. Do not wait for agents to send you details, pursue them.

43. If you are buying a house or property at the auctions, your limitations are many - in the United Kingdom a 10 per cent deposit must be put on the table immediately upon closure of the deal and you must buy within the stipulated number of days (usually 30 days) or else you will face a certain number of consequences including losing the property. Therefore the counsel would be to inspect the property before the auction day where possible to ensure that as much as possible you do not inherit tenants who could cause all kinds of problems (encumbrance etc.)

44. Buy homes at the bottom end of the market; most of them just need a simple face-lift.

45. A one bedroom flat is ideal to quickly rent out. One or two bedroom apartments are always a winner. There is always someone somewhere looking for such apartments.

46. When buying from auctions, make an offer before it is published. The chances are that you will save a lot of time, trouble and having your heart pounding on the day of the auction.

47. The rent and the mortgage of small apartments are usually in line with each other. Therefore because you did not get much rent does not matter as long as it covers the mortgage.

48. Look at the house from the point of view of the tenants - the house you are buying on auction for rent. Is it near schools? Is it in a quiet neighbourhood ? Is there an availability of public transport where it becomes necessary?

These are some of the principles that help in investing and increasing, if you desire to make money.

-9-

THE MANAGING

What motivates your desire to have money? When do you feel you have enough to carry out your motive? These questions inform why and how you must manage your resources once God begins to provide. I suppose being free from money worries, being able to choose how you spend, what you spend, what you use for the service of the Lord is behind your desire of what you trust God for.

We already know that wealth cannot buy happiness; it only improves the quality of life. The improvement is not because it can buy new joy and peace but because it can take away some worries off your mind. It is important to manage your money so that the fear of the unknown, the fear of failure, or of losing it is taken out of your life.

However, management requires a clearly defined plan, a working plan. Within the limit of that plan you must ask yourself questions: how would you feel when you achieve £1 million net worth? What difference will it make when you move into your new home? How would you see yourself the day you are totally debt free?

You would probably need to create a worksheet that shows you what your net worth is. **At the top of it, list all your assets and their value in pounds or the currency of your nation:**

⇒ Real estate

⇒ Various investments, as in stocks and shares

⇒ Savings

⇒ Retirement accounts as in pension schemes

⇒ Business interests

⇒ Intellectual property

⇒ Other assets and their monetary value, total value.

Then list your liabilities:

⇒ The mortgages

⇒ Car loans

⇒ Personal loans and credit card loans.

Total your liabilities. Deduct your liabilities from your assets. Assets minus liabilities equals to current net worth.

Select your methods of investing

Some people's investment method is the stock exchange; they are ready to buy into stocks and shares. Whatever method you choose must be the one you know you can commit the time and effort to learn. You must take full responsibility for the financial consequences of your decision. You must have very clear goals in your mind when you start managing your money.

Whatever method you choose must be with 100 per cent commitment. Whatever method you choose must be one where you end up blaming others for mistakes. If it goes wrong you cannot say "my stockbroker made me do it". Whatever method you choose must not be overridden by the emotional desire to get wealthy quick or else there might be times when you need to off load a method of investment and yet your emotions lead to you being over-cautious. For example, if you buy shares and it go down once in a while, It might just mean it is time to cut your losses.

WHY YOU MUST INVEST

1. Good years must pay for bad years

In Pharaoh's dream, the good years were meant to handle the bad years. With good management and the wisdom from above, Joseph was able to make good years pay for the bad years. In your case this is possible where you can delay your gratification and put away a lot of your moneys in pension funds.

The bad years are the yearning years, the years when the body is not as physically fit. You should never have a zero month. It would be a wise action to practice what I call the double tithe. Give 10 per cent to God in the tithe and learn to put 10 per cent into your future in your investments. The servant who was described as the profitable one in the Bible was the one who had maximised and multiplied what was given to him.

God uses seed so it can become trees. Learn to understand that what you have in your hand is a seed of tomorrow's harvest.

2. Good years must pay for bad years

Clearly define what the purpose is for your pursuit of financial increase. It could be the ability to handle and prepare for the famine years of old age, the famine days of being inactive because of downsizing or change in the industry. There are times when people have trained in certain specialised areas and suddenly find that they cannot get a job.

3. Creating wealth will help you to avoid prostituting yourself so you can be a lender and not a borrower

The interesting thing about life is that those who have monies in high yield accounts are always hoping and praying that interest rates will rise so that they can get more value for their money but borrowers are always praying that interest rates will fall so they can pay less interest on the monies they have borrowed.

4. You must invest because God has given you the power to get wealth

But thou shalt remember the LORD thy God: for it is he that giveth thee power to get wealth, that he may establish his covenant which he sware unto thy fathers, as it is this day. Deuteronomy 8:18

That power began from when you were a child but particularly strengthened when you got born-again. Did you know that a new born baby whose parents put £100 in an account which attract 3.95 per cent interest monthly would in 25 years have £10,000 in saving. Investments must be done in order for people to have more for the promotion of the kingdom of God.

5. To leave an inheritance

What beauty it would be for you to leave an inheritance for your children, endowments for a school, university or properties, stocks and shares for the ministry you believe in.

6. To start and perpetuate generational blessing

We have covered this adequately in the previous chapter on making wealth.

7. Providing for a future of comfort

Nothing puts more wrinkles on people's face than money worries. When you have anxieties about the tuition for your children's   college, your retirement, it will cause stress on your home. The   provision for a future of comfort includes taking responsibility for your finances.

WAYS OF SAVING SMARTLY

Having taken the decision to manage your finances, you must start with your cash flow. Imagine the scenario again where a man is on a salary of £25,000. The actual salary that hits his account is 60 per cent with all deductions taken. Imagine that this same man has outgoings and bills to pay. Being a believer, from your cash flow the first thing should be to bring the tithe. Having put God first you cannot be last in the things of life.

Bring ye all the tithes into the storehouse, that there may be meat in mine house, and prove me now herewith, saith the LORD of hosts, if I will not open you the windows of heaven, and pour you out a blessing, that there shall not be room enough to receive it. Malachi 3:10

The next will be that the money should go into your interest accounts. It would not be in your best interests to immediately dissipate your cash to all your various creditors even though you need to pay them. You need to ensure that the money stays with you for some time before it is released to those who you owe. That way the money works for you before it goes out.

You need to begin to reduce whatever is a liability and increase the things that are assets in your life

Shop around for the best interest rate account that also gives you all the flexibilities and access without undue penalty particularly when you need the money.

1. Clear the credit card debt

If you are in dire straits and have owed but now want to begin to manage money, you cannot be saving while you have major credit card debts. Clear the debt out and see your clearing of the debt as a form of saving, particularly because credit card debt is a liability and not an investment debt. It is not leverage.

The rule of recovery really is "Clear the debt, budget and then save." If you owed £4,000 on a credit card and you have a similar balance in your savings account, at the time of the writing of this book the interest rate possible on your money in the savings account is 4.75 per cent while credit card debt in the United Kingdom for the same amount would average about 18.5 per cent. Using the money that only brings 4.75 per cent interest to pay off is probably one of the smartest ways of saving.

2. Have a standing order for money to go instantly to your deposit account from the current account or vice versa

Today many people tend to leave a lot of money in their current account. Except for recent adjustments current accounts tend to not attract any interest and if they do it is minimum. Saving smartly would be to give your bank standing instruction that bulk monies in your current accounts which come in either through savings, direct payments i.e. salary should only leave a minimal balance while the bulk is moved to your high yield interest account.

3. Look for a stock tracking account and save in it

A stock tracking account basically means that it is used against the best performing stocks. So you are indirectly trading in the stock market with your money. Imagine a woman in her 20s who saves £100 monthly in a stock tracking account until her 30s and stops. If the money continues to perform relatively well, when she is 60 she will have £1.3 million handed over to her.

There are several smart ways to save; it does not always take having a large lump sum before one can. For example if you save £3 a day in a high yield account (assuming a constant interest rate of 4 per cent) you would have saved £100,000 in 40 years. A second example is if you save £27.75 a day in a high yield account (assuming it remains at a constant interest rate of 4 per cent) you would have saved £1,000,000 in 40 years. Saving smartly could be things as simple as taking the money you spend daily on coffee, say £1.50 and putting it in an account. At the end of the year your daily money for coffee will give you back £390.

High Yield Account

Managing money must go beyond putting money in a savings account. You must learn to look out for high yield interest accounts. Never be afraid to ask the bank, they are there to serve you and make your money work better for you. Savings is money accumulated by economising, while investment is putting out money for a higher return.

In order to manage your money you must assess the damage you have done to your finances. Form the habit of going through your statements. It is interesting; the jury is still out on what the percentage is of those who take the time to read their statements. Take the time to look at what you also owe before you know what assets you have.

4. Cut down the non-essentials immediately

Until you hit the bottom you sometimes never want to do this. However it is important to recognise the fact that some things are not as important as the emotion and value we have attached to them.

5. Budget for everything

Do not go for major shopping i.e. Christmas without a budget. Make allowance for major expenses that are coming when budgeting. Remember all your major expenses and make allowances for them.

6. Do not overdraw from your bank account without authorisation

In the United Kingdom authorised overdraft attracts around 20 per cent interest that is very high in itself. However unauthorised overdraft attracts about 30 per cent interest.

7. Study the kind of bank account you have

What are all the benefits? What are the perks? Is there a charge on your current account? Is there any payment of interest on your current account? If there is none ask for one that has interest on the monies you have in the current account and what minimum deposit is required for the interest to be added.

8. Switch your mortgage to a cheaper lender

Once you have taken a mortgage it is important to realise that it might be possible to switch to another lender who will be charging you lower interest rates although you must watch out for the penalties of moving your mortgage.

9. Spread the big expenses over several months or weeks

You need to have a balance/ equilibrium to your finances. Have the ability to predict a coming expense that may be large and therefore find a way to spread it across.

10. Do not economise what you put into your pension so that you can rest in the evening of life

In certain instances in the United Kingdom, there are people who do agency jobs which therefore means that there may be no pension attached. It would be wise to take a personal pension scheme, which is flexible and mobile, which you can take with you wherever you go and can put money into.

11. Cry out for help when you are in debt

Unpaid bills may end up in a bad credit reference and creditors may not be favourable to you. Switch your   credit

19. Dress your money up in work clothes

Put running shoes on your money. Let your money go out to work for you. It is interesting that many families have monies lying in idle places doing nothing. In the United States for example, the treasury department reports that $134 billion are unaccounted for. It probably could be some bills of $5 or $20 left in various bags, boxes and pockets and not given work to do.

20. Be insured

The Webster Dictionary describes insurance as, "An act, business or system by which pecuniary indemnity is guaranteed by one party as a company to another party in certain contingencies as of death, accident, damage, disaster, injury, loss, old age, risk, sickness or unemployment."

It will usually carry a consideration of an amount to be paid, the sum that the insurer has agreed to pay in regard to all your current, specified contingency. If your job has a certain degree of exposure to injury it would be wise to take accident insurance. You do not want to be lifting heavy loads and your back snaps, your employers are not playing ball and then, you have to depend on others for food.

The one that is also similar to that is casualty insurance that is, being insured against losses from accidental causes. Take out life insurance; it is important to realise that you are consecrated for a second, third and fourth generation. Life insurance basically gives your family something to hold onto if you were to pass on suddenly.

Endowment insurance basically means that for you to survive beyond a certain age you can cash the insurance yourself and if you were to pass on before the date of the endowment, your heir may cash the insurance.

Fire insurance covers damage that is likely to be done on your property or business.

Unemployment   insurance might be a smart kind of insurance to take out in these days of downsizing and cut downs. It gives a guarantee of payment on the part of the government for an extended period when such a person is not in employment. It is contributed to by the employee and his employers.

Health insurance takes away your worries as to the availability of adequate health care were you to fall ill suddenly. It could be applied for use in certain hospitals.

21. Budget

A budget is a guideline that helps you to divide into certain groups the kind of money you are ready to allocate to expenses for each period of time. When budgeting you must take on board the various things we have highlighted about making and managing money. So the budget basically is the tithe, the tax, the national insurance, the mortgage, the car repairs, feeding, the bills in the house i.e. electricity, water, medical bills, all standing orders that are spread over the year, insurance, debts, miscellaneous, investments and savings. All these must be put against your actual income and deducted from it.

Why should you budget?

Budgeting helps you to track your spending so that you stay within your limit card debt or any other debt to a cheaper lender until you get it all sorted out. Some people are loyal to a certain credit card. Credit card loyalty may not work for you while it is working for the people you owe.

All monies, gifts and change belonging to your children should be put in an account that is probably connected to the stock exchange so that it makes more for them, so they have something when they are growing.

12. Stabilise your expenses to be in line with your level of income

Break away from being part of the credit generation who are spending monies that are not available because invisible money is so easily accessible today.

13. Spend less than you earn

It is interesting how that when people's salaries are increased they tell themselves "now I can afford to buy this CD". Unfortunately once they do that life seems like nothing changed. It is smart not to move your spending to keep up with your income. If you cannot handle a little, much will not come.

14. Recognise the challenge you may be facing financially

If it is spiritual then through prayer and obedience to God, shut the door on the enemy who is attacking your finances. It is not difficult to know if it is a devourer. It seems like something somewhere wants to impoverish you and take you back under the spirit from which you have been set free. You must learn to keep your deliverance from it.

15. Subsidise your income

If you on a salary learn the importance of creating wealth, that many streams get their water to the sea. There are spare hours to your life, maximise them and do something else that brings money.

16. Be practical to be profitable

God will always start you with something small so if you get that right, you will increase on every side. Your ability to manage £100 affects the £1,000 level. The £1,000 level affects the £1,000,000 level.

Look for your predominant gift area and stay there.

Your passion is meant to work for you. Your strength is where your blessing lies. Look for it, develop it and let it begin to bring in everything you need in life.

17. Protect yourself, your assets and the future through various insurances

While the believer does not expect evil yet it is important to realise that somebody else may be planning it and will be executing it. Car insurance is mandatory, not because you are a bad driver but because somebody else on the road may not plan to drive properly and with care.

18. Live below your income

You have nothing to prove to anyone. If you live in a rented apartment and more than 30 per cent of your income goes on rent you are spending too much. You are living in a house you probably cannot afford. Take something lesser until your income level improves. Maybe when that happens you might even be in a place to buy yours.

Budgeting helps you to control your cash flow, your outflows compared to your savings and investments.

It helps you to choose where you spend money so that you are not buying on impulse.

Budgeting helps you to manage your emotions also and to create a future of greater gratification. It helps you to prioritise on what is more important. Budgeting helps you to be realistic about what you can and cannot do. Once you start budgeting you know what your limits are.

How to budget?

Let it reflect your true position; do not plan for the monies that are not in your hand. Only a bird in the hand is worth two in the bush. Let it reflect where you want to be at a given time.

Budgeting should mean that you are already living your dream and you are enjoying where you are on the way to where you are going. State all your income on it and deduct all your outgoings. Both direct and indirect income needs to be stated on it, so that you know your actual income.

The budget must reflect the comparison of your income versus your outgoings, your expenses. Keep detailed records of what you spend your money on. This is one of the reasons why the budget is important.

Where income exceeds expenses you establish a control system to stop the temptation of wastage, that control system must be to increase your investment level. On the other hand if your expenses exceed income, you need to take measures to change things around.

22. Have a good pension scheme

Investigate what pension scheme is available that will help you beyond the amount your employer's pay into the scheme. Pay some money personally in addition within a pension scheme. This would be a smart move particularly if you live in an economy where monies that go into a pension scheme are not taxable by the government. What a pension scheme does for you is to allow your good years to work for your lean years.

-10-
THE MULTIPLYING

We cannot end this book without a chapter that helps to understand the need to keep the flow of money and how to make it happen.

PROVOKING GENERATIONAL BLESSINGS

One of the characteristics of nations, cities and communities that are poor is that people who have previously known a certain degree of financial increase have not perpetuated their blessing. They have robbed the next generation of their contribution. A man has a capacity to either leave a curse upon his children to the third and fourth generation, or a blessing.

> *Keeping mercy for thousands, forgiving iniquity and transgression and sin, and that will by no means clear the guilty; visiting the iniquity of the fathers upon the children, and upon the children's children, unto the third and to the fourth generation. Exodus 34:7*

What distinguishes the righteous man from the unrighteous is what the righteous man leaves.

A good man leaveth an inheritance to his children's children: and the wealth of the sinner is laid up for the just. Proverbs 13:22

God reacts when we walk in disobedience and sometimes it may result in the bloodline of blessing being cut off, for the pipeline to carry the currency of blessing we must recognise why God made you to live for the purpose of releasing blessings into generations to come.

Multiplying the money God puts in your hand therefore means that you are not robbing your children or grandchildren of your contribution to their future. Every generation must leave the world a better place for their children. It is God's intention that you perpetuate generational blessings. This is why in effect, everything God gives you is in seed form so that you have more in your hand than meets the eye. It is left to you to turn the seed to a harvest and then leave seed for your children that will then provoke their own harvest.

God is interested in your future, He is interested in your ability to maximise life. He is interested in your material blessing. He invented all things and wants to make them open to you.

Beloved, I wish above all things that thou mayest prosper and be in health, even as thy soul prospereth. 3 John 2

The blanket rejection of the material world does not help us in the multiplication of money. We must embrace the truth that God made everything for us richly to enjoy, manage and also multiply for the others.

The earth is the LORD's, and the fulness thereof; the world, and they that dwell therein. Psalm 24:1

God incarnated His spiritual ideas into the material world so that a beautiful, natural world reflects to us the realm of the Spirit. The things we see are a mirror of the mind of God; they are a mirror of the Spirit realm, at least at the time He created all things, He declared it to be good before man began to destroy it.

Multiplying wealth therefore means leaving something in the family. All lasting wealth comes from the family unit and is built from generation to generation. That is why you must tie together every concept in this book. Develop your skill, increase your hourly worth so that you do not live just to make ends meet but to leave enough for the generations to come.

We will not hide them from their children, shewing to the generation to come the praises of the LORD, and his strength, and his wonderful works that he hath done. Psalm 78:4

God is interested in generational blessing. He is our Father and we are His. That is why everything He does is connected to the family structure. When He created the first man, He created the family around him. When He would come to save us, He sent the Last Adam who is His Son. Everything He does is for generations. Whatever blunts our understanding of the need to not just work to meet our needs but to perpetuate blessing cannot be from God.

Every good gift and every perfect gift is from above, and cometh down from the Father of lights, with whom is no variableness, neither shadow of turning. James 1:17

Generational blessing is being able to raise your family and give them godly values. It is being able to come into an understanding of the difference between wealth and riches. Generational wealth is teaching your children that riches are perishable assets that Christ warned us not to depend on.

> *Lay not up for yourselves treasures upon earth, where moth and rust doth corrupt, and where thieves break through and steal: Matthew 6:19*

This book is not about the mere acquiring of riches, it is learning to be all round wealthy towards God, man and generations to come.

Riches are possessions; wealth can be ideas or people. A man who has a great and godly family around him is already wealthy in relationships. Riches are what we possess, wealth is what we are. The man who only lives for himself and does not think of his children and grandchildren is a generational thief. He has done everything for himself and has not built a bridge for the future.

Satan fights the family hard because the destruction of a family is the destruction of generational blessings. The weakness of the family is the weakness of generational wealth. If your family can be ruptured it means that the pipeline that should carry the continuous flow has been ruptured and therefore the blessing may be stained. God made it clear to Abraham from the Word, that stewardship is for money and its wealth by governing his family righteously was a key to making His covenant to Abraham possible.

If you tie every teaching in this book together you will come to the understanding that perpetuating generational blessing, multiplying money in the light of what God said to Abraham is:

⇒ Receiving an inheritance.

⇒ Preserving and building the inheritance.

⇒ Passing that inheritance to future generations.

> *Now the LORD had said unto Abram, Get thee out of thy country, and from thy kindred, and from thy father's house, unto a land that I will shew thee: And I will make of thee a great nation, and I will bless thee, and make thy name great; and thou shalt be a blessing: And I will bless them that bless thee, and curse him that curseth thee: and in thee shall all families of the earth be blessed. Genesis 12:1-3*

> *Lo, children are an heritage of the LORD: and the fruit of the womb is his reward. As arrows are in the hand of a mighty man; so are children of the youth. Happy is the man that hath his quiver full of them: they shall not be ashamed, but they shall speak with the enemies in the gate. Psalm 127:3-5*

Faithful stewardship from a biblical point of view therefore has within it the need to manage the wealth and blessing that God brings. It also has within it the recognition that you cannot claim to deeply love your children and yet leave them with indebtedness. You cannot claim to deeply love your children and yet consume everything you made in your lifetime.

> *Let thy work appear unto thy servants, and thy glory unto their children. And let the beauty of the LORD our God be upon us: and establish thou the work of our hands upon us; yea, the work of our hands establish thou it. Psalm 90:16-17*

Every thinking and action you carry out with that which God provides must not be for the short run. You must make up your mind that the curse of the lack of generational wealth brought by your great grandfathers stops with you and the perpetuation of blessing starts with you. It is interesting that today's great economies are driven by high indebtedness and consumption instead of savings and investments. What this does of course is to raise a generation that is cursed by poverty and a people who are dependent on the state. It is such a state that also runs the school system, that educates our children to be job seekers, to maintain the grinding mill of the world without them being perpetuators of wealth.

TRAINING YOUR CHILDREN

Some might argue that yes, one wants to leave an inheritance for his children. However what do you do if you have raised prodigal children? Because truly, some wealthy people have left their inheritance for prodigals.

> For there is a man whose labour is in wisdom, and in knowledge, and in equity; yet to a man that hath not laboured therein shall he leave it for his portion. This also is vanity and a great evil. Ecclesiastes 2:21

However, you must recognise that part of the perpetuation of   generational wealth is the raising of godly children. I would rather salute a woman who as a single parent has raised godly children even though she left no money for them to inherit. After all, in certain instances riches gained quickly through inheritance may be lost quickly also.

An inheritance may be gotten hastily at the beginning; but the end thereof shall not be blessed. Proverbs 20:21

So let us build our family units because a nation's economic prosperity is based upon it. It does not matter how much a nation boasts to have. If it has a high divorce or illegitimacy policy, if it has a tolerance for abortion, if it causes its people to pay high taxes, to go into indebtedness, debt equity structures, civic and corporate indebtedness, the nation is also a poor nation that is not perpetuating generational blessing.

The first way to measure the economic wealth of any nation is not its GDP (Gross Domestic Product) or GNP (Gross National Product), rather it is the rate of improvement or regression of families well being in that nation. After all, the very word 'economics' itself comes from the Greek 'oekonomics' and it means 'household management'. So the 'let's spend it' attitude which people portray is a one generational thinking attitude. Generational blessing requires strategic planning.

Any enterprise is built by wise planning, becomes strong through common sense, and profits wonderfully by keeping abreast of the facts. Proverbs 24:3-4 (Living)

HOW TO MULTIPLY MONEY

Keep the currency flowing. The word 'currency' is often used to describe money. It also brings the picture of something liquid. It can either flow or the flow may be blocked. The Webster Dictionary defines currency as "currency subject to abnormal administrative restrictions usually in the interests of controlling foreign exchange." The one who can determine the flow of currency the most is you. If it is not flowing you will not get the fullness because something is blocking the flow. We sing the song "Praise God from whom all blessings flow". That in effect shows us that there is a currency of blessing that flows from God. The only thing that stops it from reaching men is men.

WHY THE CURRENT STOPS FLOWING?

Money may not be multiplied because of many of the things we have covered; however along with these could be laziness, the wrong people in our life, bad habits, our own money fears, stinginess in our attitude towards those whom we should give: God, our parents, the poor or ministering to the man of God. The flow of currency may also sometimes be influenced by our expectation. Imagine two men who want to get water out of a water hose, one coming with a cup and the other coming with a gallon container, they will go with different levels of flow.

Keep the currency flowing by being involved in the creativity of your finances. Check out investment matters and ensure that nothing is hindering your flow. Creativity helps increase.

Ask yourself questions like, What can I do to increase the flow? What can I do to be one of those perpetuating blessing? Why am I focusing more on my looks than what I make for investments? Why am I more into buying and surrounding myself with the toys of life? Why do I always think that somebody somewhere, particularly the big brother called government owes me something? Why do we always wait for grants? Why have we not asked questions like: should I keep seeking for jobs or creating jobs?

So to keep the currency flowing you must learn to own things and not just work for it. The currency must be kept flowing also by not doing anything illegal.

It is the blessing of the Lord that makes you rich without adding any sorrow. Keep the currency flowing by living within your means. If you must use leverage as we have argued earlier, use it only as it helps to increase your asset base and as soon as it is possible off-load every indebtedness including that of investment.

Once resources begin to come your way; resources include skill, a blessing, strategic persons, being noticed and being introduced to opportunities. Take advantage of it and use it to multiply your income.

Recognise that everything God gives is in seed form. When God wants to build a house He will give you the earth so you can dig the dust and build with it. To have trees He will give you seed.

1. Become financially literate

When I was in primary two my teacher taught us a song. The summary of it was, "Money was made to be spent." That seed sown into my heart was the only financial education I had in the whole of my school days. With such misinformation, a shaky foundation was laid for a life that was lacking in financial intelligence.

a. To be financially mis-educated is to make statements like "I will never be rich."

b. It is to be taught to write good resumes and to find a good job, not to create one.

c. Financial mis-education will teach you to write strong business proposals that will create jobs for others and profit for companies, and not have to create something for your future. When we were young, the few instructions we were given regarding finance were only negative warnings. We were reminded, "Money does not grow on trees." We were warned not to get into any form of indebtedness including investment.

d. The financially illiterate are always reacting emotionally, not working with financial intelligence. As we have said in other chapters every time you allow your emotions to do your financial thinking you are likely to make mistakes.

e. Multiplying money requires that you be adequately informed and continue to inform yourself on how to make money and see it increase.

You must ask yourself how you will put your brain to work instead of asking how you can afford things. Educate your mind to know that being poor and being broke are not the same thing. If you are broke it is a temporary thing, but poverty is a forever problem until you break its power as we have seen under the chapter relating to mindsets. You must educate yourself to know that multiplying money is necessary because money is a form of power and once you have it you have the ability to respond.

A feast is made for laughter, and wine maketh merry: but money answereth all things. Ecclesiastes 10:19

f. You must understand your need to be informed on matters of money; your need to be informed on stocks, investments, commodities and purchasing because it makes you victorious, particularly in areas where people would want you to be ignorant. Your understanding of money gives you the confidence to know that even if you are lacking in supply you would have developed the skill for making more and therefore you are not afraid. You just know the right step to take to make more.

g. You must inform your mind to know that it is not enough to just think positively but rather to be educated to know how to make money.

h. Educate your mind on how to multiply what is in your hand instead of being angry with your boss, job or spouse.

i. Educate your mind to go for the best to invest until you breakthrough, to fight until you win and to give it all it takes to make a difference.

j. Educate your mind to use the ideas being dropped in your mind to solve problems instead of always looking to just get a job.

k. Educate your mind on how to put your money to work. One of the characteristics of the wealthy is that even while they are not at work their money is at work either in some company in which they have bought shares or some investment in which they have made a commitment. And believe me they watch carefully before they make such investments because only a fool and his money are soon parted.

l. If you have to go to financial seminars that you hear of in town, if you have to go to real estate seminars or any area of interest that increases your financial capabilities, do so.

Make sure you do not stay ignorant. You can never rise beyond the level of understanding you have in any given area. You cannot walk with a light that is not available to you.

m. Educate your mind and allow the knowledge you gain to make you passionate, to make you desirous to win and to provoke a godly anger in you.

n. Educate your mind not to have to work to make money but to only work because you love to.

o. Educate your mind to know that part of true wealth making is to find one thing you love to do, that you are passionate about and be willing to work at that thing even if they would not pay you for it.

p. Educate your mind and continue the process even if it takes a lifetime to master the area of your specialty. Just stay at it; in the words of Nike "Just Do It".

q. Educate your mind to recognise that money is neutral; it is a tool in your hand for achieving your purpose. You must not bow at the altar of mammon but rather money must work for you.

> *No man can serve two masters: for either he will hate the one, and love the other; or else he will hold to the one, and despise the other. Ye cannot serve God and mammon.*
> *Matthew 6:24*

r. You must make yourself priceless so that no one can own your soul and no employer can buy you.

s. Part of the process of education is to get professionals to advise you and ensure that they are worth the amount you pay them. Do not go for cheap ones but rather even if it costs a lot to hear a man speak into your life, just ensure that what is shared will make you move forward in your ability to multiply money.

There are people who are slaves to money, who obey it and do what it wants. But there are those who by reason of insight and enough educating of their minds have learnt to use money and multiply it. You must join the latter group by seeking for every insight and knowledge that makes you multiply it and not make it a master. Inform your mind; what is in your head determines what comes to your hand. So stop playing and start working. Do not live in denial. Recognise mistakes you have made and recognise what steps are to be taken to get into all that you want and all that you have to be.

Jesus told the parable of the men with talents. This story is a lesson in educating one's mind. The master of these men knew them and their ability. He knew who had the capacity to manage only one, who had the capacity to manage two and five respectively. The ones who had the ability to manage it put their money in places of upward investment and assets while the man who did not know how to manage hid it and turned such a great investment into a liability.

Certainly by the time he brought it out when the master had come, it had not retained its original value. If it were in today's world it would have actually fallen below its true value because of the rate of inflation in certain economies. We do not know but this man may have been a victim or product of today's kind of schools that are designed to produce employees, not employers - the financially illiterate, not the financially literate.

t. It is important to gain all insight of finance that will make your money multiply so that as we earlier said, you can leave something for your family.

u. Educating your mind includes learning to calculate what your money is making wherever it is and moving it if it is not multiplying. That is what makes a difference between the rich and the poor. Poor people gather around themselves what only consumes from them: cars, furniture, electronics, clothing, credit card debts and other challenges, while the truly wealthy continue to increase their earning capacity by putting much of what they have in asset building ventures.

In the chapter "The Making," we have covered ground on real estate. This has great potential for the future. One of the major steps towards a financial future is to buy real estate.

Real estates does not lose its value as soon as you get home. Real estate increases your asset base. Real estate may be slow but continues to keep your money working for you. Real estate makes money your employee that goes to work while you are asleep.

v. Money is a workforce that never needs to sleep, does not need to be fed or take a break. If you are in the early days of trying to make and multiply money, do not go for the big things - big house, big car, big expense. Rather put this in asset building ventures

The rich man's wealth is his strong city: the destruction of the poor is their poverty. Proverbs 10:15

w. The greater the wealth in your hand the greater the need for accuracy also or else everything will fall apart like the house of cards. However, as you keep studying and learning how to invest, as you keep seeking for information wherever you can find it, you will become an informed man.

2. Create multiple streams of income

The man who is well informed in matters of finance will also recognise that money is like rivers. All rivers head for the sea. Wisdom should prevail as you create the atmosphere for financial increase. There are other methods for making money. They may not deliver as high a return as real estate investment, even though, as you can tell from this book I have a bias for real estate. Yet some ventures may bring quick profit though limited; but the consistency of the flow helps you to be able to maximise your money, have quick returns from various places and not have to wait a long time.

3. Multiply money by re-orientation

If you have children start teaching them how to manage finance and how to multiply money. Do not repeat the mistakes that were made with you. Your parents were probably not good communicators on the subject. Give your children the opportunity to learn early. Open bank accounts for them, teach them something about the stock market, show them how to buy stocks and shares and help them early to develop the mindset and thought pattern of wealth making. If you do not do that your children will be caught in the trap of what you went through. They will find themselves talking and dreaming of financial well-being but with no financial intelligence and therefore repeating the mistakes of their fathers.

Show your children how that raising the value of their hour is more important than being particular about how much they are paid. Teach them that it is more important to be able to be financially free, to multiply the finances in their hand, than to be thinking of the wonderful things money can buy. Help your children to be free from financial fears. Deal with their money fears. Help them to have confidence in God and to know that as long as they remain in the will of God and have the right attitude toward money, seeing it as a tool for glorifying God, it can never hold them in bondage.

Educate your children to know that if they had good grades and a good degree it should not be in order to work for anyone or to be able to get a better pay cheque. Rather it should be in order to make a difference, to increase their personal value in everything they do. Let them know that a life dictated by the size of pay cheque is a false life and an unhappy one.

And he said unto them, Take heed, and beware of covetousness: for a man's life consisteth not in the abundance of the things which he possesseth. Luke 12:15

Your children are not alone; they are surrounded by other children who probably will not have the opportunity to get the kind of financial education available to yours and who therefore may influence the way your children think. However, continue to challenge them to recognise the need to perpetuate generational blessing to increase their assets and not their liabilities.

The rich ruleth over the poor, and the borrower is servant to the lender. Proverbs 22:7

THE RESULTS

King Solomon paints down for us what God will do when we begin to work at multiplying what God has provided for us. However, before we refer to Solomon we must remember that David calls us to the wealthy place.

Thou hast caused men to ride over our heads; we went through fire and through water: but thou broughtest us out into a wealthy place. Psalm 66:12

The wealthy place is the place of multiplication, where you multiply the assets, blessing and favour in your life. It is where liabilities decrease and eventually disappear. Multiplying your finance would result in

1. Being ransomed from the bondage of lack

Poverty and shame shall be to him that refuseth instruction: but he that regardeth reproof shall be honoured. Proverbs 13:18

2. Financial increase

Wealth gotten by vanity shall be diminished: but he that gathereth by labour shall increase. Proverbs 13:11

Increase will follow as these principles are applied.

3. Generational blessing

A good man leaveth an inheritance to his children's children: and the wealth of the sinner is laid up for the just. Proverbs 13:22

The man who chooses to multiply what God has brought will leave an inheritance for the children. After all, none of us was called to live only for his own generation.

4. A crown for the wise

The crown of the wise is their riches: but the foolishness of fools is folly. Proverbs 14:24

What else is there to crown the life of a man who has chosen to build assets with the blessings that God put in his hands? The favour and the blessing of God become the crown upon such a man's labour.

5. A strong city of protection

The Bible describes wealth as a strong city, a walled city or a rich man's protection, truly so because it wears off sickness, increases value, removes certain ungodly associations and stops all the terrible experiences of the poor.

6. Influence and power

Wealth maketh many friends; but the poor is separated from his neighbour. Proverbs 19:4

We cannot deny that along with the blessing of the Lord comes a certain degree of influence and power so that such people are able to speak and their voice is heard.

7. The ability to honour God with abundance

Honour the LORD with thy substance, and with the firstfruits of all thine increase: Proverbs 3:9

The whole purpose of the blessing is that we might also be a blessing but the cheapest of all our reasons for having wealth and blessing is because God is seeking for conduits through which the currency must flow.

ENJOYING ABRAHAM'S BLESSING

E d Montgomery said, "How often have some many others waited for some deity to pour out great blessings of wealth without any effort on their part? To wait for any higher power to give us anything is the first indication of weakness. We were never created to receive without effort, to gain without trying, or to achieve without struggle."

As I try to tie together what this book intends to communicate, the story of the patriarch Abraham becomes my best possible way. From him we understand certain cardinal truths that:

Wealth is what you accumulate, not the things you consume.

And Abram was very rich in cattle, in silver, and in gold. Genesis 13:2

Abraham's case shows that divine empowerment, not luck, a mere inheritance, advanced degrees, or the level of intelligence you have, can be the basis of great wealth and blessing. Furthermore we see this from his lifestyle, his handy work, his planning, and the perseverance he expressed in the face of opposition not dealing with strange relations.

And the LORD said unto Abram, after that Lot was separated from him, Lift up now thine eyes, and look from the place where thou art northward, and southward, and eastward, and westward: Genesis 13:14

Self-discipline, commitment and living right influenced Abraham's ability to create wealth. When the crisis came and Abraham had to separate from his nephew, he was willing to take the land that was of lesser value, work it up and expect it to become better. The setback he was experiencing did not stop his ability to continue to create wealth. The creation of wealth is not possible if you are dependent upon a monthly salary, particularly if you are so dependent that you could not survive without a pay cheque.

Abraham was a symbol of true wealth creators. He rarely displayed what he had.

By faith Abraham, when he was called to go out into a place which he should after receive for an inheritance, obeyed; and he went out, not knowing whither he went.

By faith he sojourned in the land of promise, as in a strange country, dwelling in tabernacles with Isaac and Jacob, the heirs with him of the same promise: Hebrews 11:8-9

Abraham recognised the power of ministering through his tithes, offerings and whatever God provided for him. The scriptures express the fact that he was a giver.

And Melchizedek king of Salem brought forth bread and wine: and he was the priest of the most high God. And he blessed him, and said, Blessed be Abram of the most high God, possessor of heaven and earth: And blessed be the most high God, which hath delivered thine enemies into thy hand. And he gave him tithes of all. Genesis 14:18-20

Like most world creators, he was not out to impress people by the kind of house he lived in and the neighbours he had. True wealth creators do not make that their primary drive. He was not after showing off that he could buy the best clothes in town. True wealth creators do not even wear their title like some would choose to do.

From the scriptures we see that Abraham was a cattle-rearer. Many times you will find that when people choose to manage what God has provided for them (they may be office workers, welders, contractors, farmers or other kinds of businesses) blessings follow, particularly if they recognise the power of the creation of wealth and that the creation of wealth is not exactly a matter of trying to be a job seeker.

We have taken the time to write about the need to have a good work ethic in order to make and to manage the finances God provides. Nothing works like work. Nothing works like being a good and fastidious investor. It is important to look for the things that appreciate and put that which God has provided into them.

It is also important for you to be confident of who you are in God and the abilities deposited in you without any sense of arrogance or pride. Once your godly self-confidence is gone through the window, it will be difficult to build anything that is tangible and can make impact.

You do not have to inherit wealth or have a big start to make any impact. It might just mean that through your initial work you saved enough to buy your first property and from that one you generated enough deposit for other properties.

Whatever you do, let your motives be right. Financial independence, the need to know joy, the need to be secure without a sense of dependency on others, the need to have enough to use in serving the Lord, touching the needs of people around the world; if these are your motives then certainly nothing can stop you.

NOTES

MATTHEW ASHIMOLOWO MEDIA

www.pastormatthew.tv	www.amazon.com
iTunes store	Kindle store

Ghana: Motivational Media Limited:
P.O. Box AN 19792
Accra-North.
Tel: +233 243 69 00 71

Nigeria: 13 Oki Lane, Mende, Maryland,
Lagos, Nigeria.
Tel: + 234 1 899 8822/8833

Namibia: Unit 20 Gutenbergplatz.
Werner List Str.
Windhoek. Tel: +264 61 30 62 66

South Africa: 5 Star Junction, Unit 14, 174-177 Zandspruit
Corner Beyers, Naude & Juice Street,
Honeydew, Johannesburg
Tel: +27(01)17 94 68 78 / +27
(0)826 30 63 05

United Kingdom: KICC Prayer City
Buckmore Park
Chatham, Kent ME5 9QG
Tel: +44(0)845 130 3471

USA: Matthew Ashimolowo Ministries,
P.O. Box 470470,
Tulsa, OK 74147-0470.
Tel: +1-800 717 0571